SKILFUL

SQUASH

D1511453

First published 1990 by
A & C Black (Publishers) Limited
35 Bedford Row, London WC1R 4JH

ISBN 0 7136 5749 9

A CIP catalogue record for this book is available from
the British Library.

Acknowledgements
All photographs by Stephen Line except cover
photograph and photograph on page 85 courtesy of
Action Plus Photographic and photographs on pages
18, 19, 20, 21, 22, 25, 27, 28, 33 and 34
reproduced by kind permission of Heather Wallace

Line illustrations by Taurus Graphics

Printed and bound in Great Britain by
William Clowes Ltd, Beccles and London

CONTENTS

INTRODUCTION

The appeal of squash

'Squash is so simple game' is a quotation frequently associated with the great Khan dynasty of world-class squash players. But for most of us it never seems quite so straightforward.

Squash is, nevertheless, a game of simple pleasures. It seems to be universally popular to hit a ball against a wall with a racket, and there is an intense pleasure to be had in playing a head-to-head competition which produces a winner. It is also becoming increasingly popular to take vigorous exercise such as squash provides in order to improve one's general state of health.

However, the area of the game that is perhaps considered least is the tactical expertise that leads to the full enjoyment of these pleasures. Much of the experience necessary to play a tactically sound game of squash can be learned at any age and need not be the preserve of those in the first bloom of youth.

The sport of squash is thoroughly enjoyable for those who make a firm commitment to playing it. It is certainly not necessary to be a physical paragon such as some coaches envisage. An opponent of a similar standard to you is sufficient to ensure a highly competitive game of squash, while if your opponent is slightly better or worse than you the score can sometimes tend to reflect a one-sided match. Do not despair at this; the desire to persevere and learn more will see you through.

There are many different levels in the game of squash and whatever level you play at, you can seriously enjoy competing and meeting a wide cross-section of people socially. It is a well-known fact that business people use

1 Two legends of the game, Geoff Hunt (Australia) and Hashim Khan (Pakistan), swap ideas about the game of squash

squash clubs as a vehicle for furthering their business interests, and this is made easier because of the compact nature of the sport; it is quite easy to fit in a game over a lunch break. Even a hectic person's schedule will usually have a spare hour which is sufficient for a good forty-minute session, shower, change and a sandwich on the way back to the office. Squash seems ideally suited to the modern lifestyle.

Fitness considerations

Before taking on a full squash calendar you should ensure that you are physically in good shape. Much has been made of the so-called 'killer squash' angle in the tabloid press, and it is right to take all reasonable care so that nothing untoward happens. A vigorous activity like squash does put a tremendous strain on the heart and it is important to build up gradually to your full pace. This applies equally to each match you play – not just to your first efforts to learn the game from scratch. You should always be eager to consult either a medical expert or your club's coaching professional should you have any real doubts about what you are doing.

Pride can sometimes cloud this issue, particularly for somebody who is ultra-competitive and who will put himself through excessive physical discomfort to achieve the right result. This is not wise or beneficial to the long-term enjoyment of the sport, because to try and play to maximum capacity without the appropriate form of warm-up and preparation is a shock to the system and is asking for trouble. This is not meant to sound gloomy, but after all squash is only a game and there is no sense in doing something that is foolhardy, and which endangers life and limb. It is never so vital to be a winner that you put yourself at risk; there is always the possibility that tomorrow you will be that winner anyway, without the danger.

It is a good idea to play squash regularly, not only to maintain and improve your fitness, but also to improve your standard of play. The more you play, the sooner you will improve your skills, so that eventually you will be able to avoid heavy physical demands with good racket work.

Styles and standards of play

Squash should always be fun, and at the point when it ceases to be fun you should seriously ask yourself why. Different players have different styles, and each new opponent poses a new set of problems and challenges. Some will hit the ball hard and low to make the ball travel fast and furiously to its destination. Some will play with great variety of pace, placing the ball in the corners. Some will be defensively orientated and seek to run down all your strokes in the belief that sooner or later you will be forced to make an error. Some will be attack-minded and seek to make winners at every available opportunity.

Each different style of play you encounter will require you to make adjustments in your own game to cope with the problems. Hopefully, by skilful use of your own armoury you will be able to absorb your opponent's game plan, impose your own and ultimately triumph. All the answers will have to come from you alone, because when you walk on court nobody else can do it for you. Squash can be likened to a physical version of chess. The different strokes represent the pieces with their set possibilities, and it is up to each individual to maximise the effectiveness of these pieces according to his own potential.

Learning from others

It is important to talk squash with other players and in particular those who are of a higher standard than you. Their knowledge of the game will be most instructive and you can learn a great deal from their tactical methods and their overall sharpness of play.

Coaches

Most clubs have their own coaches, and, so that you are able to keep motivating yourself to improve, it is worth investing in some lessons. A good coach will be invaluable to you in the competitive jungle of league and tournament squash because you will need his help when things are not going well. Never be afraid to

2 England international Neil Harvey seeks guidance from the author

seek advice from your coach – there is a great deal to be learned and he can prevent you from developing bad habits. He will also be able to introduce you to suitable playing and practice partners, and to advise you on which tournaments to enter.

When selecting your coach, try and make sure that he is not going to place too much emphasis on physical conditioning. He should concentrate instead on the technical and tactical aspects of the game, and he should make your sessions fun. The choice of coach is entirely up to you, but it is advisable to pick a coach who will be sympathetic to your particular style of play.

Clubs

All clubs have some form of internal league or pyramid structure which you will join on becoming a member. Most clubs will insist that you start at the very bottom unless you come highly recommended or have a proven track record. Working up from the bottom might seem a little frustrating, but it does ensure that you have plenty of matches. Once you have attained the higher reaches, don't hide away to protect your reputation but continue to join in and face the challenge of each new opponent.

Clubs put on their own calendar of squash and social events over and above the regular diet of matches in the internal leagues. These might include a knock-out, a doubles tournament, a pairs match or a handicap event, all of which should give you the opportunity to compete against players of a higher standard in a good social environment. There will also most likely be a calendar of friendly fixtures for the club's social team against other local clubs.

When you begin to win a few matches the club will no doubt want you to play in their representative teams which compete in the local and regional leagues. Team squash is very popular both because of its social nature and because of the competitiveness involved in the task of trying to become league champions, win promotion or avoid relegation. Leagues run for most of the squash season and are interspersed with tournaments held at the weekends.

Making squash work for you

The following chapters assume that the majority of readers are already hitting the ball quite competently and are most likely playing to a reasonable standard. However, I make no apology for examining some basic aspects of technique, because even at higher levels of play, when things go wrong it is important to go back to the sound fundamentals of stroking the ball, footwork and concentration. Every step forward that you make should incorporate these basic principles of technique. In this book I have looked at each of the strokes and tried to give information that is geared to their use both in matches and in more general tactical contexts.

Note Throughout the book players are referred to individually as 'he'. This should, of course, be taken to mean 'he or she' where appropriate. Similarly, the instructions throughout the text are geared towards right-handed players and left-handers should simply reverse these instructions.

THE HISTORY AND DEVELOPMENT OF SQUASH

Harrow school is credited with the initial development of the game of squash. This came about because boys queuing to play rackets could not get on to a court and so would use any available wall to practise with racket and ball while they were waiting. Gradually squash took hold and the sheer simplicity of the game attracted the attention of many future players.

Certainly, squash has some notable advantages over other racket sports. For one thing the ball does not travel very far away, requiring a break in play to go and retrieve it at the end of a rally. Also, being an indoor sport the weather has no effect; this is important both for countries like the United Kingdom which have very poor weather conditions, and for countries like Pakistan which have very hot weather. In the early days there were some open air courts, but these have been replaced to stop the ball disappearing out of the court and to prevent interruptions due to inclement weather.

Squash was introduced to Pakistan by the armed forces who built squash courts in the country because it was a very popular leisure-time activity. Other countries which have traditionally played squash include Australia, New Zealand and Egypt. There are many countries newly taking up the challenge of squash, including Sweden, Germany, Spain and France in Europe, and Japan, Singapore, Hong Kong and Malaysia in the Far East. The South American tournament circuit is blooming and squash is also being played more and more in North America and Canada.

World-wide there are around 12 million squash players utilising 37,000 courts. The number of players is even higher if we take into account those individuals who do not play regularly. The figures show that squash ranks in the top drawer in terms of the most popular sports.

The boom in the sixties and seventies in the number of courts being built seems to have reached something of a plateau. However, while not so dramatic as the building boom, the development of teaching, competition and club management during the late eighties has provided the game with the solidity at grass roots level that it needed.

In 1980 the professional and amateur distinction was abolished and the game was declared open. This did not have a radical effect on the sport, but it did help create an overall unity.

EQUIPMENT

Courts

The court has to be of the dimensions laid out in the rules of the game. However, courts differ from club to club and while these differences may not be glaringly obvious, they are often sufficient to throw you out of your best form on a bad day. If you are going to play on a different court for a match that is particularly important, then take the trouble to go and have a practice on the court earlier in the day. This will help you to see if you can work out the different qualities of the court and turn them to your advantage.

Some things to look out for are the lighting (this may be brighter or darker than you are used to) and the speed of the ball off the front wall. Also, the side walls may grip and hold the ball, thus changing the angle at which it leaves the side wall and also making it

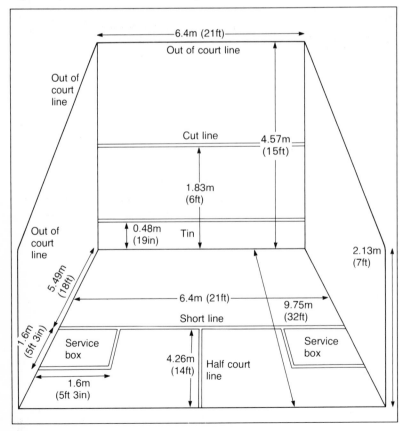

Fig 1   The dimensions of the squash court

3 A portable squash court sited in the Royal Albert Hall, London for the 1987 World Team Championships

more likely to cling to the wall for a winner. If the side walls are very smooth and shiny the ball may well skid off this surface, while the walls in the back corners may keep the ball low, making it difficult to play out of the back corners. Finally, the ball may be very bouncy or the court may be exceptionally hot or cold.

All of these factors will require you to adapt your game to suit the conditions. Do not be alarmed – these problems are not so pronounced as they may seem, but awareness of such differences will be useful in trying to steal an immediate advantage over your opponent.

The floor

There has been a good deal of controversy recently concerning the floors of squash courts. It is important that the floor is not covered with a sealant, since drops of perspiration can turn it into a lethal surface on which you will slip and slide. This is patently unsafe; if players are moving at top speed they can lose balance and take a tumble, perhaps falling head first towards

a wall. This is definitely to be avoided.

If you are confronted with this type of surface and have no option but to play, tread very warily at first and gain your confidence before risking your full speed. You could suggest to the club management that they consider sanding down the floor to the natural wood surface in order to make the floor a safe one on which to play.

The squash ball

Speed

The four balls which are in common use range from the blue dot, which is the fastest and has the highest bounce, to the yellow dot which is the extra slow ball with the least bounce. The red and white balls rank in between the two extremes. The yellow dot is the ball most

11

commonly used for tournaments by the world's best players. This does not mean that it is the right ball for every player; there are occasions in particularly cold weather when a faster ball makes for a better game. The professionals will quite often use faster balls in practice to simulate the conditions of major tournament finals where the court may be made excessively hot by additional lighting for television purposes. So do not hesitate to change the balls to a faster dot if you are not getting the bounce that allows you to have a good game.

Colour

Squash balls come in two different colours – black and green. The green ball was designed not to mark the squash court walls, so it is manufactured from a different rubber compound to the black ball which does leave quite a severe mark on the walls. However, the green ball, because of its slightly different rubber compound, has never quite achieved the same consistency of bounce as the more established black ball and tends to be faster and a bit of a 'flier'. Also, the green ball does leave a green sheen on the walls, although this is not quite as much an eyesore as the black mark. The difference is that the green mark is more difficult to clean than the black one, which is removed simply and cheaply with soap and water.

Therefore, if you do have the choice, remember that the black ball plays more consistently and makes for a better game than the green. There are some clubs that insist on the green non-marking ball, so while having to adhere to the rules, try where possible to use the ball that most suits your game.

The racket

The wooden racket is near enough obsolete, having been replaced by the different types of graphite composite racket. These composite rackets are manufactured from a variety of materials, including graphite, kevlar, boron, aluminium and so on, all of which are thought to benefit the player in some way.

The same tests hold good for selecting a graphite composite racket as for a wooden one. You should always test out a racket to ensure that it feels and plays right for you. If it feels good in your hand and plays well then the chances are you have bought the right racket. Many of the racket manufacturers produce rackets with different shaped heads and frames. Strings are more often made of synthetic material these days, mainly because the quality of synthetic stringing has improved to such a degree that the difference from natural gut is barely discernible, but also because synthetic strings generally last longer.

Grips

Handle grips are now being produced in a variety of materials and the choice comes down purely to personal preference. I choose towelling grips because I feel they give me a grip on the racket that suits my needs, but I do have to change these grips very regularly as they become worn and hardened with perspiration quite quickly. It is not a big task to change the grip, so it is worth changing to a fresh one quite frequently. You must make your own choice, always putting control over your racket first.

Clothing

There is no set clothing for squash but the choice seems to lie somewhere between the fashion conscious tennis clothing and the more casual and comfortable athletics clothing. There is no doubt that tennis clothing looks smarter on the squash court, but the more physically orientated squash players contend that athletics clothing is more functional for the rigours of a squash match. Whatever you choose to wear, ensure that you have freedom of movement and feel comfortable. There are no hard and fast rules any more – the British Open tournament regulations are usually the strictest and they allow either white or pastel squash clothing. There are still one or two older and more traditional clubs that do enforce a strict whites only code, but that is swimming against the tide in this day and age. Remember, clothing should not be so tight that you suffer discomfort or find that you cannot make overhead volleys with ease.

It is vital in colder climates to have a good warm track suit. Fashion can dictate what it will, but the main requirement is that it keeps you and your muscles warm until you are working hard enough to be able to remove it. It is also vital to protect cold muscles to avoid pulls, tears or strains. When you have finished playing, before making your way back to the changing rooms put on your track suit again. This ensures that you do not cool down before you are ready to shower and change. These are all basic, sensible precautions to safeguard your health and ensure the continued enjoyment of your squash.

Footwear

Always take care in choosing your footwear – your feet are a vital part of your game. Blisters or other foot ailments can put you right out of the game, but they are all avoidable by taking

sensible precautions. Choose squash shoes that fit properly; if you want to wear an extra pair of socks for added protection you will probably need a slightly larger shoe than if you are only going to wear one pair of socks.

Sports shoe manufacturers are now generally making shoes lighter so that as a player becomes heavy-legged and tired at the end of a hard match, he will not be overburdened by his footwear. They are also removing or lowering the high tab at the back of the ankle. This tab was once thought of as a support, but is now generally held to be medically unwise because it puts pressure on the Achilles tendon. Some squash shoes provide arch support.

TECHNIQUE

Technique is of paramount importance when it comes to picking up a racket and stroking the ball with any degree of control. Poor technique will inevitably lead to errors. Therefore, certain basic elements have to be dealt with before progressing to the act of hitting.

The grip

It is possible to pick up the racket and hit the ball using any old grip, but to do so with skill requires a good, sensible positioning of the hand on the handle. In simple terms, if your opponent offers you his racket by holding the head and positioning the shaft and grip of the racket towards you and you then 'shake hands' with the racket, this will give you the correct grip. A 'V' shape should be noticeable, formed by the thumb and forefinger on top of the handle and pointing up the length of the racket. The grip is firm but not too tight and the fingers are slightly spread so that the racket feels comfortable in the hand. The forefinger is in front of the thumb. This orthodox grip will give you access to all the different strokes of the game and will also allow for maximum ball control.

Errors

Common errors include gripping the racket too tightly with the forefinger inside the thumb, and either opening or closing the face of the racket by incorrectly aligning the 'V' shape along the top of the racket shaft. Ideally, the alignment should appear just slightly to the left of centre. Slight variations are not catastrophic but they are the source of errors; for example a grip that is too tight can lead to the arm prematurely suffering fatigue in a match, causing the result to go the wrong way.

The swing

This will allow you to bring the racket head through the ball with the maximum efficiency, ensuring accuracy of stroke so that the ball goes where you want it to. Remember, however, that since two players are in close proximity within a squash court, a large or uncontrolled swing could lead to accidents.

The swing is one continuous movement of the racket and arm, but it is made up of three distinct phases.

1. *The back swing* The back swing prepares you for the intended stroke. Early preparation is ideal as it disguises your intentions; late preparation reduces the stroke options. The swing commences with the arm raised, holding the racket in a vertical position above the head with a slight bend at the elbow.
2. *The down swing* The idea is to generate speed of racket head movement which is then transferred as momentum to the ball at the point of impact. The greater the momentum, the more power will be generated in hitting the ball. Obviously, where less power is required you do not need a large back swing. The racket face must remain open throughout the swing and travel through a horizontal plane to meet the bail in the same plane.
3. *The follow-through* This begins the moment the ball is struck by the racket.

4 and 5   The 'shake hands' racket grip. Note the 'V' shape made between the thumb and forefinger at the top of the racket

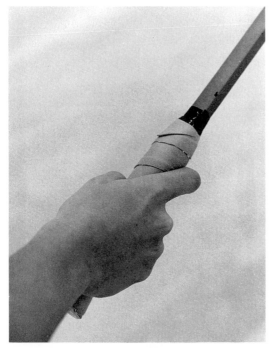 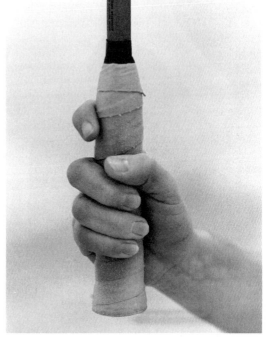

6 and 7   Spread the fingers comfortably for maximum control of the racket

It finishes with the racket in a vertical position above the head and over the opposite shoulder from which the back swing started.

The elbow should always be slightly bent because a full, straight arm swing is excessive and dangerous. As long as the racket starts and finishes above your head, then generally the swing should be safe and out of your opponent's way.

The cocked wrist

This is the means whereby the racket head is controlled to arrive in the same striking position for each stroke. It is achieved by tilting the wrist of the hand holding the racket to an angle of 90 degrees to the arm when it is parallel to the ground. This is maintained throughout the swing and although it sounds ungainly it is quite commonly used in practice. Failure to cock the wrist can be a source of errors in stroke-making. It is possible under pressure to strike the ball

8 The great Jonah Barrington shows grip variation by shortening the racket so as to dig a good stroke out of the back corner

10   Alison Cumings (England) does not control her follow-through here, leaving her compatriot Lisa Opie to face an unpleasant experience

9   Australian Rodney Martin demonstrates perfect position for the backswing

11   Phil Kenyon (England) is determined to play his stroke despite the crowding of his opponent who then has to take evasive action

without cocking the wrist, but this is not to be recommended and is mainly used by experienced players who are having to improvise.

The straight drive

You will need to master the basic elements, that is holding the racket comfortably and ensuring good swing, footwork and body position, before progressing to the difficult task of dealing with the ball. Should there be difficulties at any stage, then you must return to these very basic technical ingredients, because most mistakes tend to stem from a malfunction in one or more of these areas. These basic elements are the same for all the different strokes covered in the following chapters, although there will be small adjustments to be made in certain cases.

The two strokes fundamental to the game of squash are the forehand and the backhand drive. The forehand drive is hit adjacent to the right hand wall of the court and the backhand to the left hand wall.

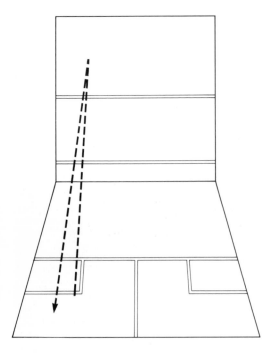

Fig 2   The straight drive

The forehand drive

For the forehand drive the left leg acts as the leading leg and the left shoulder points towards the side wall on the right. Ideally, the right leg will be situated at a comfortable distance from the leading leg so that at the moment of striking the ball the player is in a balanced position. Thus the only part of the body that moves is the arm holding the racket, and the body position acts as a pivot. This positioning

12   Backswing position for the start of the forehand drive

13 Above   **The downswing**

14 Right   **Leaning into the stroke**

15   The point of contact with the ball. Note how the player keeps the knees bent and maintains a well balanced position to deal with the low ball

16   The follow-through

17   The racket finishes high above the head with a view to avoiding any contact with the opponent

18   Sarah Fitz-gerald (Australia) perfectly poised for the forehand drive

should provide the best possible chance of accurately stroking the ball. The ball is struck at the point where it is in line with the knee of the leading leg. This will obviously vary according to your opponent's shot and the prevailing conditions.

Adjustments such as bending the knees to lower position or stretching to reach have to take account of all the possibilities. Footwork and body position will improve with practice and with match experience. The two seem to be linked; certainly, under pressure both the

footwork and the positioning deteriorate, causing matches to be lost through an excess of errors.

The backhand drive

The backhand drive is the reverse of the above although the same principles hold good. The right leg is the leading leg and the right shoulder points towards the left side wall. Good balance makes the stroke easier.

19 Above **Backswing position for the backhand drive**

20 Right **The downswing**

21 Leaning into the stroke

22 The point of contact with the ball. It is essential here to keep the head still, watch the ball and maintain good balance

23 The follow-through

24 The racket is kept well under control and finishes high above the player's head

25 Susan Devoy (New Zealand) displays her powerful backhand drive

Application

The ball should ideally be struck so that it clings to the side wall and bounces the second time in the nick at the back wall. Obviously, by varying the height at which the ball is struck on the front wall in proportion to the degree of power used, you can ensure that the ball alights in the same place. For example the ball struck at service-line height will require much less power than the ball struck 46cm (18in) above the tin. It is your responsibility to ensure that this power to height ratio called pace is understood and utilised to the best advantage. Suffice to say at this stage that the drive to a length is the most common opening gambit in any rally and without it you will be at a disadvantage.

The drive to the back corner places your opponent in the most difficult part of the court, so work hard to master this stroke on both sides of the court. It is more difficult to respond to the backhand than the forehand because although the backhand is not as 'natural' a stroke, when it is executed well it does tend to be more accurate, positively clinging to the side wall. The forehand, while generally easier to execute, tends to be played with less caution and thus with less accuracy. Take care with both of these strokes as it is only by good driving to the back corners that the rest of the strokes in the game will become available to you.

Remember, therefore, if in doubt drive the ball into the back corners. There are always other possibilities but this is the simplest and the best. This way your options are utilised at the correct stage of the rally, giving a stability to your play.

Cross-court drives

There is very little technical difference between the cross-court drive and the straight drive. The very best players will keep the body position and the footwork more or less the same, thus providing the added bonus of disguising the intended direction of the ball. The actual difference lies in the fact that the cross-court drive is hit at an earlier point in the ball's path, that is when it is in front of the leading leg as opposed to being in line with it.

The cross-court drive is the stroke that comes most naturally in the game of squash as it is dictated by the swing of the racket. However, it is also the most common source of untidy ball control, being the end-product of last-minute preparations to hit the ball while under pressure. Like the backhand and forehand drives, it is a stroke that has to be played with care; the ball can very easily be struck through the midcourt area, which is the central dominating position of your opponent. It is important to concentrate on hitting the ball well wide of your opponent or he might volley from the middle of the court. Many rallies will end with poor cross-court drives being vollied away for winners.

The target area for cross-court drives should be the side wall around the service box. However, the shot can be hit straighter and aimed at the back corners, providing that the stroke has sufficient height to avoid any volley by your opponent, or that he is already out of position.

The strategic objective of both the cross-court and the straight drive to the back corners is to move your opponent away from the key midcourt area by making him retrieve the ball from the corners. This means that you can then legitimately take up your position in the middle of the court.

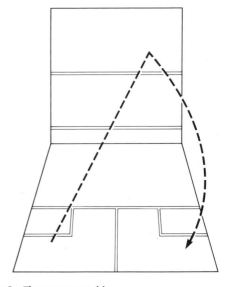

Fig 3 The cross-court drive

26 The forehand cross-court drive played in front of the body, open-chested

27 Backhand cross-court drive

28 Susan Devoy (New Zealand) demonstrating her best stroke, the straight drop, against Martine Le Moignan (England)

Drop shots

The straight drop shot is potentially the most lethal stroke in any player's repertoire. It is aimed as low as possible over the tin and angled in towards the side wall, ideally in order to hit the 'nick'. Few players achieve real mastery of this stroke. It should stay low in the front court because of its lack of pace and it is designed to drag your opponent from the depths of the back corners to the front court at breakneck speed, so that even if the stroke is not an outright winner it will at least be energy-sapping.

The drop shot can be played on both the

29 Preparation for the drop shot. The player keeps his knees bent and his weight well forward

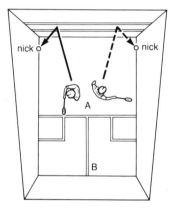

Fig 4 Drop shots are most effective when played in area 'A'. They may also be played from poor length shots in area 'B'

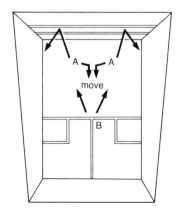

Fig 5 Having played the drop shot, move away so that you do not obscure your opponent's view of the ball

30 The ball is stroked gently but the racket is held firmly

31a and b The player keeps his head down and uses a shortened follow-through to take the pace off the ball

forehand and the backhand sides of the court. The swing is similar to that of the drive but is shortened to provide the necessary feel for controlling the softer touch on the ball which will slow down the pace. Some players can play the drop shot with no pace from exactly the same swing as the drive. This is very difficult to do but is also even harder for an opponent to read.

The straight drop shot is the most effective because the ball has so little distance to travel before it is dead and even if it is played poorly there is a degree of protection from the side wall. The cross-court drop shot does not have such an immediate effect unless it drops perfectly into the nick. Played badly the cross-court drop shot can provide a set-up ball for your opponent, and therefore a free hit with the possibility of finishing the rally.

Tactical usage of these two variations is very important and I will deal with this in a later chapter. Generally, however, the backhand side of your game will produce better drop shots; most players seem to play the stroke on the forehand with great carelessness and inaccuracy and since more care is needed with the backhand technique, greater accuracy should result.

The kill

The 'kill' is derived from the basic drives, the only difference being the area of the front wall at which the stroke is aimed. Unlike the drives, the kill is intended to stay short at the front of the court. There is no difference in power – it is the accuracy involved in aiming the ball as low over the tin as possible that distinguishes it. The straight kill is angled into the side wall nick, which in itself helps to hold the ball in the front area of the court. The cross-court kill is also aimed at the nick and is the most commonly used variation. The kill looks spectacular and is highly effective when combined with a stroke to the nick.

If it is possible to hit the ball hard enough it will 'squash' on to the front wall and literally just fall off it. This stunning shot is the best example of the kill. Unless you can master this shot it will not be easy to make the ball stay short unless you are successful in hitting the nick. This stroke is most effective when your opponent is anticipating a drive to the back corners and is therefore lying deep in the court. You may then use the kill to finish the rally while your opponent is out of position and unable to retrieve.

The technique for killing the ball short is to

32 Jahangir Khan (Pakistan) preparing for the backhand drop shot

hit down over the ball at the top of the bounce. Obviously, there is a danger of hitting the ball too low, and because the margin of error is so slim you should be careful to avoid hitting the tin. It is essential that you practise this stroke regularly.

Angles

There are many different angles, all of which have different uses for different situations in the rally and for different areas of the court.

29

The same basic elements of technique hold good for all of them, but these must be allied to a good knowledge of geometry. By definition the angle is a drive aimed at the front wall on a course via the side wall.

To learn the angle it helps to face the side wall with your back to the front wall and consciously point the leading shoulder to where the ball will be struck on the side wall. Strike the ball firmly and use the angle of trajectory from the side wall to throw the ball up on to the front wall. If the ball comes off the side wall at a shallow angle and is struck high up the side wall on to the front wall, the stroke will not need to be hit with great power. Correspondingly, the more acute the angle and the lower the ball on the side wall, the greater power the stroke will require.

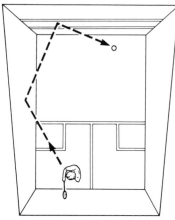

Fig 8   An angle played from deep in the back of the court (backhand)

Figs 6 and 7   Positioning and footwork for the angle

Ideally, you should aim to play the angle low over the tin. However, there are two distinct uses of the stroke. The first is purely defensive, intended to get the ball out of the back corners. It is not always possible to keep the ball low in this situation; it is more likely that you will be grateful just to see the ball on the front wall and the rally continuing.

The second use of the stroke is in attack, where the prime requirement is to keep the ball low over the tin, and where the ball may travel as far as the opposite side wall, alighting in the nick on its first bounce. A second attacking winner occurs when the ball, hit at a shallower

Fig 7

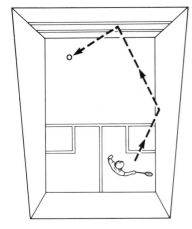

Fig 9   Defensive use of the angle

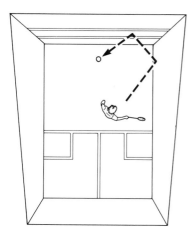

Fig 10   Attacking use of the angle

The short angle

This is sometimes called the 'trickle boast', in reference to that part of the court where the angle is played. The stroke is always played in the front of the court whether on the forehand or the backhand, and it is usually used to disguise the player's intentions. It is an attacking stroke played off a weak stroke by the opponent, and the element of deception, combined with the fact that the ball is kept low over the tin, should make it a winner. No power is required for the stroke and footwork is often intentionally unorthodox to add to the element of disguise. However, orthodox footwork more often provides the best possible disguise.

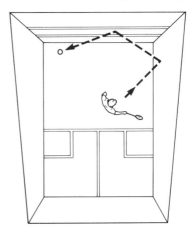

Fig 11   The short angle

The high angle or skid boast

This is a combination of the angle and the lob: the ball is struck firmly, more like an angle than a lob, while the height aimed at is that of a lob. The ball is hit high up, rising into the side wall so that it is thrown on to the middle section of the front wall. The ball should land like a lob, deep in the corner of the opposite back court. The initial use of power makes the ball skid off the first side wall, but by the time it has bounced off both this wall and the front wall, it should land in the opposite corner without any pace, just like a lob.

This is an effective shot which also contains the element of surprise. It is not nearly as easy to hit this stroke on the backhand side of the

angle, bounces for the second time into the opposite side wall nick after alighting somewhere in the middle of the front wall.

The acute angle requires a slightly more closed body position than is the case for the shallow angle. However, the main aim is always to make the stroke easier to play accurately.

There are other strokes that are part of the family of angles and the following are variations on the theme.

court as it is on the forehand, thus it is more commonly used to switch the attack from the forehand to the backhand corner at the rear of the court.

The back wall boast

As its name implies, the ball is struck off the back wall on to the front wall rather than the side wall. It is usually played facing the back wall and as such is a desperate stroke – the last line of defence in an attempt to stay in the rally. The essence of the stroke lies in the fact that, although it requires little power, it is struck high up on to the back wall and then in turn on to the front wall in the same trajectory as a lob in reverse. However, because it drops without pace on to the front wall this is tantamount to a free hit for the opponent in the front of the court, as the player may well be stranded in the back

corner. As a defensive, last ditch attempt to stay in the rally it is justified – otherwise it is not.

Fig 12 The back wall boast

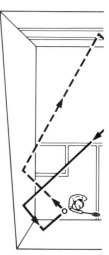

33 The author is forced to play the back wall boast in his match against Qamar Zanan (Pakistan)

Reverse angle

Most angles are played to the nearest side wall to which the ball is travelling. The reverse angle always traverses the full width of the court before striking the opposite side wall and then the front wall. The element of surprise and the fact that the ball is kept low over the tin makes this stroke a winner. Do be careful, though, not to strike the ball at your opponent. If he is rightly in the middle of the court when you aim your reverse angle from the back court area, hitting him may change the whole course of the match, and not necessarily for the better. As a consequence, you may also run short of opponents!

34   Preparation for the backhand cross-court lob

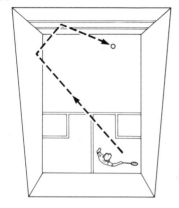

Fig 13   The reverse angle

The lob

This is one of the most underrated strokes in the squash player's repertoire. It is commonly regarded as a defensive stroke, but it is also very effective as an attacking weapon and as a change in tactics. Ideally, the footwork and the body position should be the same as for the drive, but in a defensive situation this is not always possible.

The great virtues of the stroke lie in the extreme height which it is possible to gain (as high as the court dimensions will allow) and in the lack of pace. The height should clear any possible volley from your opponent in the middle of the court, while the lack of pace should ensure that when the ball falls in the back corner it is almost impossible to dig out.

35   The player's weight is placed firmly on his front foot

36 The racket face must be kept open

37 The follow-through takes the racket high over the player's head

The cross-court lob

The cross-court lob is the most frequently used variation and is often played at full stretch from the front of the court when retrieving a very low attempted winner. It is important to take account of the out-of-court lines and to practise making the ball fall just within them. The swing does not have to be as full as for a drive to obtain the necessary height in the stroke, but the down swing will come from underneath the path of the ball and the follow-through will continue its way upwards. In rugby parlance it is a kind of 'up and under'. The racket face should therefore be kept as open as possible for this stroke.

As an attacking weapon the lob can be used to exploit any weakness that your opponent may have high up on the backhand volley, which is a difficult area in anybody's game. The lob is also deceptive; it gives the impression of being a soft touch for a powerful volleyed winner. Provided that the opponent is kept at full stretch by the lob you will see its value in your armoury of shots.

Volleys

Application

All the different strokes outlined early in this chapter can be played on the volley instead of off the bounce. The ball is struck while still in flight before it has the chance to bounce on the floor.

Both the volley and the half-volley are generally attacking plays. For example it is quite a good idea to volley a lob when at all possible, because by the time the ball bounces it is likely that, with so little pace on it, the ball will die in the back corner. The volley is therefore very useful to any player who does not feel comfortable playing in the back corners.

The volley is particularly effective because it involves taking the ball early in its flight, thus reducing the time that your opponent has to recover from his last stroke and to prepare for the next one. It is a very elementary way of rushing your opponent and therefore pressurising him into making mistakes.

38 Jansher Khan (Pakistan) plays a forehand volley which takes Rodney Martin of Australia completely by surprise

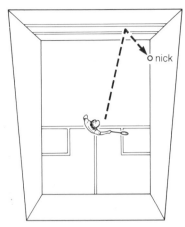

Fig 14   Volley from the middle of the court

Technically speaking, the positioning is the same as for the basic strokes. The arc of the swing must be adapted to take account of the fact that the ball may arrive at any height from waist, shoulder to overhead. Whatever the height, there is no real difference in the mechanics of the swing. It is particularly important to ensure that your footwork is good because good balance is vital for accuracy. There is no real point in volleying if you are not well balanced and you cannot be sure of an accurate stroke, as this will immediately transfer the initiative to your opponent.

Most volleys and half-volleys are struck low over the tin. This deprives your opponent of time and, allied to early contact with the ball in its flight path, should leave him scrambling to retrieve your stroke. The more practice that you can get at perfecting your accuracy, keeping the ball low over the tin and aiming for the nick, the sooner your game will dramatically improve. Good volleying will help you to become a better squash player.

The half-volley

The half-volley is the name for a stroke played immediately after the ball has bounced once; this is sometimes imperceptible to all but the most alert spectators. The stroke does not have any special function other than to get you out of a sticky situation, and it is often merely a convenient way to ensure that the attacking mood of the rally is maintained. The half-volley is a reflex action, employed when a volley would have been preferable but was impossible and when the impetus of the rally would otherwise have been lost. It involves stepping backwards to take the ball at the top of the bounce, and can also be used to get out of a defensive situation or a situation that has been misjudged. The important thing to remember is to take care with your footwork and your positioning as it is easy to end up hitting the ball into the tin if you are caught in two minds.

39   Rodney Eyles (Australia) shows good preparation for the backhand volley

The service

The service is the start of the rally and is therefore most important. Although the service in squash does not have the same potency as in tennis, it is only when you are serving or are 'hand in' that you can score. Unless you are fortunate enough to get the first service of the match by the spin of the racket you will be required to win a rally in order to serve. Do not be careless with the service; it is hard earned and you should make it count in your favour.

The service is the only time during a rally that you are able to select your preferred positioning and control the ball. It should be possible to make the most of this, as from then on in the rally your opponent will attempt to dictate your next stroke with his return. Take your time over the serve and make sure it is good. A quality service can give you the initiative, particularly if you can force your opponent into making a

weak return, leaving you to finish the rally with a well-chosen winner. Do not under any circumstances allow your opponent to hit a winner off your service.

Technically speaking, the service puts a premium on doing all the basics correctly in order to ensure an absolutely accurate stroke. Since you have the time to prepare the serve to perfection, there is no excuse for a poor effort. The following are the three basic types of service.

The lob service

This is very similar to the straight lob. The lob service is hit with very little pace high up on to the front wall at a point midway between the two side walls. This throws the ball even higher up into an arc so that it falls touching the side wall near the back wall, just within the out-of-court lines. The ball then drops without

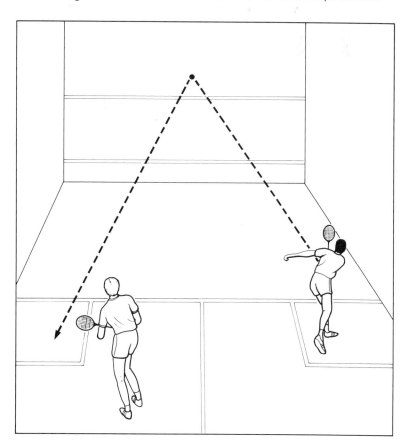

Fig 15   The service

40 Phil Kenyon (England) hitting a flat service

any pace into the back corner, virtually running parallel to the back wall. The ball should be high enough to make it very difficult for your opponent to volley and should also fall so 'dead' into the back corner that it is practically impossible to make any sort of return other than a desperate angle. The initiative then is firmly with the server for the forthcoming rally.

This service is not easy, and a poor lob will give your opponent the opportunity to make an attacking volley which, in one hit, would give him the initiative. Practising the service regularly will produce the necessary accuracy, but you should be wary of playing the shot too casually.

The flat service

The flat service is so called because of the trajectory taken by the ball. It is less risky than the lob service since it does not aim for such close proximity to the out-of-court lines. It is aimed at the middle of the front wall above the service fault-line. The service presents few difficulties for the receiving player because even if he opts not to volley, the ball should have sufficient pace to bounce out of the back corners, enabling him to make the return.

The key elements of the flat service are that it is generally a safe stroke to play at moments of high pressure during a match, and that it can be

41   Neil Harvey (England) demonstrating the lob service

relied upon to start the rally, even if rather negatively. More can be made of this service by constantly varying the angle of delivery and therefore the point in the service box at which you aim. For example some players drive the ball at the back wall nick on the full, hoping for a winner, while others aim for the opponent's body or his 'wrong side'. Thus if the service is to be received in the forehand service court, the server would opt to serve to the backhand, creating an element of surprise which may be enough to force an error.

It is an equally good idea to make the flat serve difficult to volley. This always helps psychologically because it prevents your opponent from moving to an attacking position. The secret with this service is to try to outwit your opponent by finding a service target that in some way inconveniences him and surprises him through change of pace and direction.

The corkscrew service

This is the most difficult service. It flirts dangerously with the rules, particularly those concerning foot faults and out-of-court lines and the one that designates that the service must always hit the front wall first. The corkscrew service has the advantage of being a complete surprise, and used sparingly may be enough to squeeze a point or two per match from your opponent. The corkscrew effect is achieved by hitting the ball high up on the front wall very close to the side wall nearest your service box. The ball is thrown high into the air so that it spins into the service court and hopefully hits the opposite side wall near the back wall. If this happens the spin is released off the side wall and the ball should end up running parallel to the back wall, making it impossible to retrieve. You will have to serve the forehand from the left hand service box and the backhand from the right hand side.

Your opponent should find this very difficult to volley because as well as having all the height of a lob service it is also spinning vigorously. Even if he is skilful enough to be able to make contact with his volley, the corkscrew service should cause your opponent to miscue his return. If he chooses to allow the service to come out of the back corner he should again be frustrated, as the most accurate corkscrew lob service will actually cling to the back walls.

The corkscrew service has to be hit with great accuracy on to the front wall to achieve its effect. Since this requires that great power be generated in the stroke, the backhand version is ruled out for most players. The stroke is lethal when played well, but its difficulty means that it is rarely used except as a trick shot by the professionals.

Return of service

Given that the service has to land in the forehand or backhand quarter of the court, the receiver can take up a position that gives him the best possible chance of returning the ball. This position is usually at the centre of the service court, since this makes it possible for the receiver to step forward and volley a poor service or to retreat and stroke the ball defensively out of the back corner using the angle. Remembering that it is a good tactic to make the best possible start to the rally, it is obviously better to volley the ball if you can.

The server will try to take up a position in the middle of the court in order to take control of the rest of the rally. However, a good volleyed return to the back corners will immediately remove your opponent from the middle of the court and allow you to move there and dictate your terms for the rest of the rally.

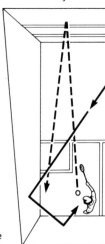

Fig 16 Return of service coming off the back wall

There is no better return of service than a fierce volleyed drive down the wall into the back corner – especially if it clings to the wall. This means that the server will have to hurry to the furthest point from his service box, aiming to arrive and make his return before the ball dies in the corner (that is providing he can scrape the ball off the wall). This return could become the bread and butter of your game, but do not be afraid to vary your returns. By doing so, you will ensure that the server is never quite sure what is going to happen to his service next, which is particularly important if his serving is not up to standard.

You need to practise a good deal in order to become proficient at returning a deep lob service out of the back corners with an accurate angle. This is never easy if the service is accurate, but remember that there are very few services that make outright winners and it is worth working on perfecting the angle and improving your accuracy until you become more confident. At the highest level very few services require the angled return, because the return can be hit straight back down the wall with a shortened swing and a flick of the wrist. This takes practice but can be done.

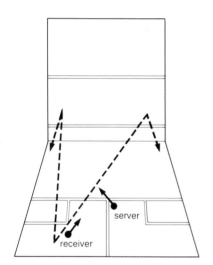

Figs 17 and 18   Short returns of service

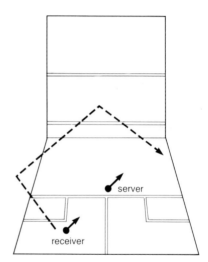

Fig 18

PRACTICES

Practice makes perfect is a very good axiom for squash technique. This chapter is devoted to a series of exercises designed to improve the skills of your game. Thus the amount of time devoted to racket and ball work will be reflected in your improved ball control. The top players regard these hours of practice as money in the bank and as good investment for when their ball control is put under the most severe pressure in a match situation. You should be able to take the following exercises and adapt them to your own needs in order to create a similar type of investment.

Ball control is vital because it allows you to select a stroke which you know will have a specific effect on the rally. However, if the execution is disappointing then it all counts for nothing. Some strokes have a very slim margin of error; for example in selecting a drop shot, a kill or an attacking angle, the ball has to be struck low over the tin if it is to bounce sufficiently low and make it difficult for your opponent to return. Similarly, the lob or the length strokes, while not going so close to the tin, none the less are ineffective if the ball does not arrive accurately at its correct destination, and may give the opponent a chance to attack the weak return.

Therefore if you work hard to master these ball skill exercises the full range of strokes will be at your disposal, allowing you to attack your opponent rather than the other way round. At the end of the day, ball skills often tend to be the decisive factor.

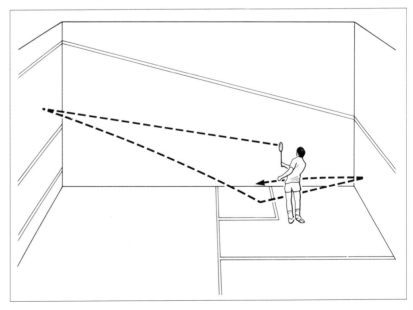

Fig 19   Service box hitting

Solo skill practices

Service box hitting

This practice is precisely what the name suggests. Take up a position near the forehand side wall just behind the service box. Aim to strike the ball on to the front wall so that it lands on the first bounce in the service box and repeat the stroke. Each time the ball lands in the service box count one point and repeat, attempting to build up a good score. Should you fail to hit the service box stop and start again, counting your score from nought. The repetitions should build up a good score and at the same time improve the accuracy and consistency of your ball control.

Initially, it is a good idea to keep the pace slow and the ball high up on the front wall. As you become more proficient you can make the practice more difficult by increasing the power of the stroke, and by not allowing yourself to strike the ball above the service line on the front wall.

Reverse the exercise to work on the backhand side wall. Through constant repetition you will grow more sure of the feel of the ball on the racket strings and more confident of controlling the ball on to the front wall.

Back wall hitting

The aim now is to hit the ball so that it bounces behind the service box and hits the back wall with sufficient force to rebound. You will then be able to hit the ball back down the side wall again to the same position just in front of the back wall.

This is another practice that demands repetition and consistency. Again, you must be hard on yourself if you are not meeting the standards of accuracy – cancel your score to nought and start counting again. The exercise is particularly useful for learning to judge the bounce of the ball in the back corners and may be repeated on the backhand.

As you become more expert in both these exercises, you can strive to hit the ball closer and closer to the side wall, eventually trying to beat yourself for accuracy by making the ball cling to the side wall.

Solo vollies

Cross-court volley

Take up a position at the centre point of the court – the 'T'. Volley drive the ball on your forehand up on to the front wall close to the backhand side wall, so that the ball returns as a corkscrew lob to the centre of the court. Then, using the backhand, volley drive the ball to the opposite end of the front wall close to the forehand side wall. Again the ball will corkscrew lob back to the centre of the court. As your consistency improves with repetition, you will need to be able to work out the power to height ratio for the ball played on to the front wall. The higher you hit the ball the less power will be required to achieve the same effect as if you hit the ball lower but with greater power. Count for repetitions and be tough on yourself.

Straight vollies

Take a short swing and, standing in the front half of the court, volley the ball at shoulder height to hit the front wall just above the service line. As you become proficient repeat the same exercise, but this time stand deeper in the court and also volley the ball higher up on to the front wall. The most difficult thing is to stand behind the service box and volley the ball overhead as you would with a lob. A good score here will demonstrate excellent ball-control. Repeat for the backhand side of the court.

You may not be able to do these exercises as a beginner because you do need quite a good degree of ball control, but once you start, good results can be obtained by repeated practice.

Pairs practices

There is little hard running to do in these practices because they are designed purely with a view to making the stroke technically correct and accurate. Sometimes one player will adopt the role of a feeder or a coach, but this is not necessary unless your partner is making a lot of errors. These exercises can easily be adapted for ball machines.

Cross-court drive/angle

Two players take up suitable positions for executing an allocated stroke. The important thing is that the players are able to practise this stroke for the greatest accuracy. Cross-court drives should be wide, low and aimed at the service box on the opposite side of the court. The drive should definitely *not* travel through the midcourt area to be vollied by an imaginary opponent.

For this practice you should start as above with the deep drive, but alternate after the first phase by using the kill low over the tin to make the ball bounce twice before the midcourt line. Your partner supplies the ball by way of practising his angles. One of these should aim to die on the first bounce off the front wall in the opposite side wall nick, while the other should be aimed low over the tin, bouncing twice in the front court area with the second bounce alighting in the side wall nick. Accuracy is of the essence

and, given that you should always know what is going to happen next and are moving only to take up the best position and to use the best possible technique, near perfection is possible.

Change roles with your partner so that you both practise cross-court drives and angles. Pride and competitiveness will make you both strive for the best possible ball control.

Cross-court lob/angle

This is the same as above, only replacing the drive with the lob. While the angle is more difficult in this exercise, it can be played on the volley, and though tricky to master this shot can be most effective.

The exercise can also be adapted to practise the service and the return of service. However, while the exercise is very useful, it tends to be disjointed as the service can only be practised at a static point at the beginning of a rally, and the return cannot set up any continuity.

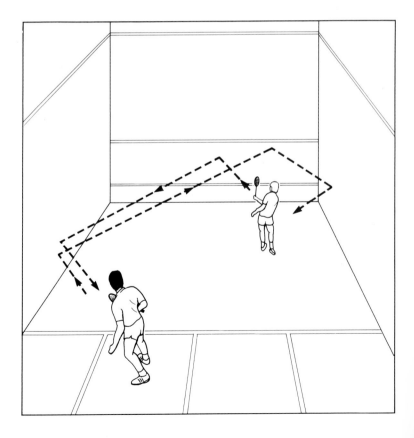

Fig 20 Cross-court drive/angle

Cross-court lob/nick

The 'lob' now becomes a pure feeder stroke to allow the partner to practise the cross-court nick. The lob should be varied to make the partner hit to the nick off the volley, off the ground or even from a drop shot. Hitting to the nick is the most attacking option and is a means of terminating the rally. The ability to make the ball hit the nick and roll flat on to the floorboards is a vital part of the modern squash player's armoury, and you should work hard to perfect this stroke. The nick is the only outright winning stroke that does not depend on your opponent being manoeuvred out of position.

Straight drive/drop

The player feeding drop shots off the drive will need excellent ball control because it is extremely difficult to take the pace off a fierce drive and return the ball with accuracy.

However, it is worth persevering because the skill would be a most useful addition to your repertoire. If you are playing the drive you should concentrate on accuracy and a gradual build up of power in the stroke.

The exercise takes place down the length of each of the side walls in turn. The person playing the drive is in the front of the court and the drop shot maker positions himself behind the service box. The drive can vary between a deep shot and a 'kill' shot, and you should experiment with the power to height ratio involved in stroking the ball on to the front wall. Don't forget to try and make the ball cling to the side wall.

The roles may be reversed and the exercise varied by the person who is on the drive playing straight lobs, and his partner responding with a vollied drop. Very high skill levels are required here, but once you have attained them the rewards will soon become obvious in your match play.

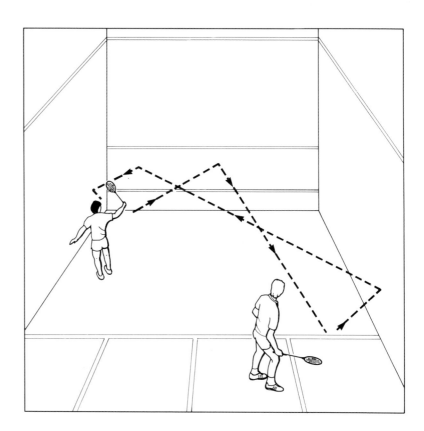

Fig 21 Cross-court drive/angle

Skill practices on the move

Thus far the practices have been static in the main. While this is good for learning to play the stroke correctly, it is not sufficient to help you deal with match situations. It is time, therefore, to introduce practices that incorporate some movement.

Straight drive/angle

This is the most popular practice routine. There has to be movement because neither of the players practising is hitting the ball back to his partner. Yet although you are moving around, you should not sacrifice your accuracy. The drives should always be deep to the back corners and as close to the side wall as possible. The angle should always be low over the tin so that your partner will have to hurry to be in position to make an accurate drive down the

wall. Experiment with the power to height ratio when you strike the ball at the front wall – remember that the pace of the ball should be such that it will die in the back corners and not bounce back into the midcourt area. The ability to judge the weight of shot is vital at the higher levels of play.

Straight and cross-court drive/angle

This is exactly the same as the previous exercise except for the addition of the cross-court drive. The player in the front of the court should differentiate between his position for the straight and the cross-court drives in order to dictate stroke selection. It is usual to alternate the two drives at first. The exercise reduces the amount of movement each player has to make because two strokes are hit from the same part of the court before the players move on to the next position.

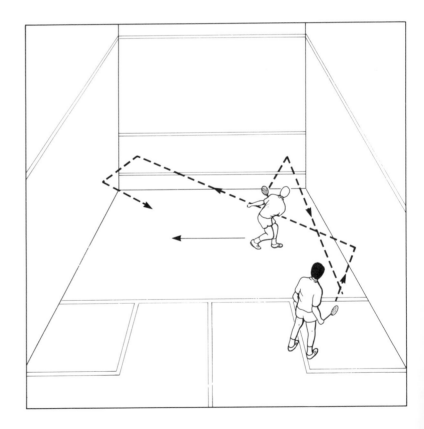

Fig 22 Straight and cross-court drive/angle and straight drop

Straight and cross-court drive/angle and straight drop

The player at the back of the court hitting angles and straight drops has almost become a feeder in this exercise, and thus he will require powers of control and accuracy. There must be a desire to assist the player at the front if the exercise is to work properly. There is a great deal of pressure on the player making the drives because he has to move with great speed in order to take up his position.

The feeder operates from a static position while his partner will always strike the ball back to the feeder's part of the court. It is important to build a good rhythm to ensure control and accuracy. This is vital for the player driving the ball as he is under the most severe pressure. Roles should be reversed after a suitable period of time as fatigue does set in; the player making the drives needs to work constructively

and not be collapsing with fatigue. The more you practise, the longer you will be able to keep it up as you become more accustomed to such pressure. Repeat from both the forehand and the backhand sides of the court.

Straight drop and cross-court lob/counter-drop and angle

This has a feeder as in the previous exercise. The feeder plays straight drop shots and cross-court lobs and remains static, only moving to clear a path for the incoming striker who is attempting to retrieve the drop shot. The counter-drop to the drop shot is straightforward enough, but covering the full distance of the diagonal part of the court is the longest and one of the hardest moves in the game.

The exercise is repeated on both sides of the court. Pay special attention to technique and do not allow it to collapse due to fatigue. If you

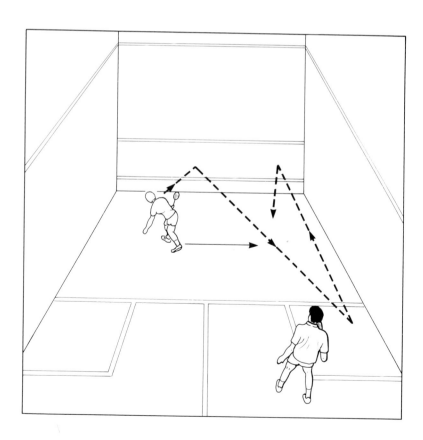

Fig 23   Straight and cross-court drive/angle and straight drop

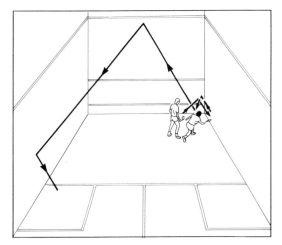

Figs 24 and 25   Straight drop and cross-court lob/counter-drop and angle

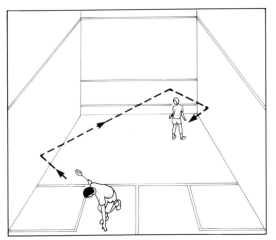

Fig 25

feel tired, reverse the roles. The tiring player can earn some respite by hitting his counter-drop or angle for a winning nick, thus creating some extra time while the feeder retrieves the ball and starts the procedure again. Accuracy here can save energy as well as symbolically representing a point won.

Cross-court lob/straight volley drive/angle

This contains less pressure work and is therefore a useful warm-up exercise. The players alternate, working through the three required strokes.

Player A makes the cross-court lob, player B makes a straight volley drive and player A then returns the ball to player B with the angle. The process becomes continuous and potentially never-ending. The exercise breaks down only with an error, making it possible to continue for very long periods of time. The movement is not so fast and furious as in previous exercises, making fatigue less of a problem and also encouraging accuracy and good technique. The exercise should be repeated on both sides of the court.

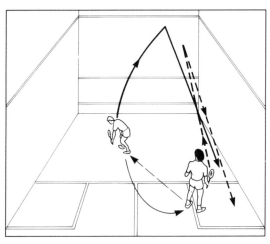

Figs 26 and 27   Cross-court lob/straight volley drive/angle

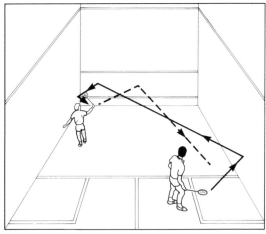

Fig 27

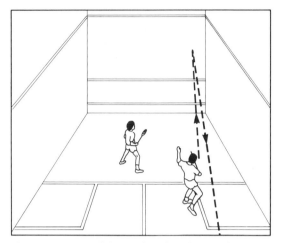

Fig 28 Cross-court lob/straight volley drive/angle

Pressure practices for groups – the double feed

This is a useful routine for teams who want to practise stroke-making under pressure. It is just as testing on the two feeders as on the player practising. The feeders will take full responsibility for making the player practise properly because the quality with which they deliver the ball determines the success of the exercise.

The feeders

This practice takes place in the service boxes on both sides of the court and involves both backhand and forehand feeders. The two feeders have a ball each and work together to propel each ball to the front wall, alternating feeds. This makes it possible for the striker to hit the ball without interruption and so build up momentum.

The timing of delivery for each stroke has to be precise and the feeder has to hit the ball with not too much pace half-way up the front wall. This allows the striker just enough time to reach the ball and hit it before it bounces twice. Fed at this pace and height, the second feeder can time his feed for the moment just after the striker has made his play on the other side of the court. There is just enough time then for the striker to move to the

other side of the court and make his next play which should be exactly the same for both the forehand and the backhand sides of the court. A harmony should develop between the three players, although this will always be somewhat an uneasy one for the striker.

The striker

The striker concentrates solely on his strokes and on his mobility – not on his errors. Any errors are to be corrected by the feeders, who must rapidly retrieve the ball and be ready to make the next feed so that the momentum is maintained. Any loss of momentum is the feeders' responsibility. The feeders are in control of the striker's work-rate and they can increase or decrease the pressure by speeding up or slowing down the time taken for each feed. It is wise to start slowly and build up gradually in order to allow the striker to find his rhythm and progress to the most difficult moves. You can keep practising even after you begin to feel fatigued; in a squash match it is often necessary to keep ball control and technique together despite the onset of fatigue.

When the striker is at rest he becomes a feeder and one of the feeders steps forward for his session. Such rotation gives each of the players a chance to rest but not to lose concentration, because there are also stringent demands involved in feeding the new striker. Ideally, a coach or a feeder should provide encouragement, technical analysis and timings for the session to help the striker who is under pressure. It is important that the start and the finish are disciplined so that the session has good impetus and concludes decisively.

The strokes

The following strokes can be practised within the same formula. They all have to be played down the alley of the side wall.

1. Low, hard drive to the back corners off the bounce.
2. Straight nick kill off the bounce.
3. Vollies off the two previous strokes.
4. Lob.
5. Drop shot. (For this stroke the feeders move

42 Susan Devoy (New Zealand) hits a backhand drive at full stretch

to take up positions close to the front wall and feed the ball by hand.)

All of these strokes should be practised on their own initially, but a typical session may finish using the above in combinations of two or three.

By alternately isolating each stroke on both the forehand and the backhand wings, it is possible to practise the accuracy of the stroke either for depth and lowness over the tin or for development of weight-of-stroke awareness (the height and pace ratio of the ball on the front wall). There is also the possibility of being able to make the ball cling to the side wall. Accuracy is once again the key element, but it is closely linked to the amount of pressure that is created by the feeders. This pressure can build up to such a degree that it is not possible, in view of the time allowed to execute each stroke, to be so accurate. It is wise to practise such a situation as much as possible. It is unlikely that you will ever be under so much pressure during a match, except, that is, if you are playing against somebody who is a lot better than you.

If the pressure practices are difficult enough then the pressure you face during a match may well seem less. Given that you will then have more time, you should be able to make your strokes accurate, thus laying the foundations for successful squash.

Competitive conditioned games

For these games you will require a partner. The games are devised to ensure that your play in a pre-selected area of the court is up to standard, and they offer a competitive stimulus to try and improve. Often, while you are isolating a particular area of your game your opponent will continue to play his normal game – this is not essential, as he can also work under the same restrictions. However, it is a useful exercise for your opponent to play normally and it does mean that he may not necessarily need to be of the same standard as you. In fact a player of a lower standard makes for a better game, since two players of the same standard tend to find the unhandicapped player winning too easily. Serving is usually the same as for a match.

The back court game

For this exercise you are restricted to hitting the ball above service-line height so that it lands behind the line on the floor of the midcourt area. Alternatively, you can dispense with the service-line height rule and practise getting the ball into the back corners from all parts of the front wall, wherever your opponent places the ball. If both players play to these rules one rally should take a very long time, so it is better for your opponent to play normally. It is not easy to win playing solely a back court game. Few winners are really possible but a good contest full of protracted rallies should result.

The short game

This is a reversal of the last game. The ball must be struck below service-line height on the front wall so that it lands in the front of the court ahead of the midcourt line. You will have to be extra careful with your ball control to avoid peppering the tin. Rallies are likely to be short, which affords good practise for the kill and the touch required for drop shots. Variety is important for this exercise and there should be evidence of short and low angles. It is difficult to make consistent winners, but it is possible to win as many games as you lose in this exercise.

The side wall game

The restriction in this exercise is an imaginary rectangle extending the full length of the side wall and the full width of the service box. The area also extends to encompass the full height of the court, but it is essentially a narrow corridor which necessitates a good degree of ball control and accuracy. There is no restriction on power or direction for the strokes as long as the bounce is within the side wall corridor. This has the effect of encouraging the player to hit the ball so that it clings to the side wall and is low over the tin, and to aim for height, depth and change of pace. Since your opponent will easily be able to patrol your restricted area, precision strokes and tactical variations are at a premium.

Playing within such confines has the effect of raising standards and cutting out strokes that are loose or inaccurate (these will hopefully become the domain of your more uninhibited opponent). It is possible to raise the quality of your play in this exercise to such a level that a clear-cut advantage is registered over your opponent. Players may use this tactic in normal match conditions, particularly when things are not going too well, since it is a destructive ploy in itself.

When playing in this area of the court always be mindful of your opponent's position and allow him access, especially if you have just made a precision stroke. Also, be prepared to restrict your swing if there is a sign of danger. This restricted game teaches you a great deal about the movement of players to and from the ball and the answer seems to be to give and take in equal measure.

It is also important to be aware that your opponent's position in the court can be controlled if you hit the ball to that area of the court which you are not occupying.

The cross-court game

The cross-court shot is the most casual stroke in the squash player's repertoire, mainly because it is so natural to swing the racket and see the ball fly across to the other side of the court. It is much more difficult to hit the ball with accuracy and control either straight down the wall or wide across the court. The definition of a good cross-court shot is that it is a stroke which it is not possible to volley when taking up position in the midcourt area.

In this game your opponent knows you are committed to hitting cross-court and will read the stroke early, forcing you to hit even wider or higher to stop him volleying your drives. This will demand greater accuracy from you than is normally required in a match.

Take care with this game – it is harder to do well than it may seem at first. Do not be afraid to explore all the variations on cross-court work.

The angles game

This is not a particularly competitive game because having to use the extra wall before the ball reaches the front wall means that the opponent has extra time to cover all eventualities and is not posed any serious problems. It is sufficient to use this exercise as a means of practising accurate angles low over the tin. It is also useful for experimenting with different ways of throwing the ball on to the front wall. This gives you the option of the shallow angle or the acute angle for the other side wall nick stroke. The skid boast is a version of the angle that will help you to push your opponent to the back corners while the reverse angles can also be used as a variation. However, by and large you should find this game hard to win.

MATCH PRACTICE

The basic groundwork has now been done and the time is fast approaching for you to move into the match arena. The basic techniques have all been covered so you should have a sufficient armoury of strokes. However, it is necessary to look at the tactical use of these 'weapons' and the preparations that are necessary as you approach the match.

Choosing a practice partner

The most obvious way of preparing for a match is to play practice matches against different and carefully selected opponents. If you know who your opponent for a forthcoming match is to be, then try to choose practice partners who are similar in their style of play to him. It is no use lining up practice partners who play a good touch game with skilful use of drop shots if your opponent hits the ball hard to the back corners.

It is a good idea to try and play with somebody who is in a better league than yourself. There is much to be learned from playing with a highly skilled practitioner who makes you earn every point. His use of tactics, ball control, speed and stamina will be an invaluable eye-opener for you. However, since it can be a depressing experience to score a heavy loss, it might be a good idea to balance this opponent with one who you know you can beat. This should keep your morale high.

Making the most of practice sessions

Remember that whatever happens in a practice match, your wins are never as good as you might like to think nor are your losses quite as disastrous. All players subconsciously tend to hold a little something in reserve for big occasions such as a tournament or a league match when there is something extra at stake. But this does not mean that you should treat your practice matches lightly.

You should always work as hard in practice matches as you do in your other sessions since they are a golden opportunity to test out your strokes in match situations. Practice matches also provide you with an ideal opportunity to experiment with aspects such as shot selection and tactical ploys which are very difficult to apply to real match situations.

It is only by meticulous work in practice matches that you can build up the confidence to use new ideas in the real big match environment. However, it is still often necessary to play more circumspectly in an actual match, because tactical indulgences can be a major source of error and you may suffer from big match nerves that inhibit your play. Thus any experimenting should be restricted to the practice court, with the big match remaining the real testing ground.

While practice matches are all right up to a point, nothing can substitute for actual match play. You need to combine match practice and regular match play, to join leagues either with a team or as an individual and to enter tournaments. There is no substitute for the big match occasion, and the more you put yourself in competitive situations the sooner you will come to terms with them.

One versus two practice

This game is designed to prepare you for a match. It is especially useful if there is a shortage of solo practice partners of a suitable standard, because two players of a lower standard can form an effective doubles pairing and give you a sufficiently testing match practice. Thus playing against a good doubles pair is similar to playing against a player of a higher standard. This is because two players have only half the court the single player has to cover and they can therefore do so easily and quickly.

You will find that this exercise makes such demands on your play that you need increased racket and ball control, speed across the court and mental alertness to contain your opponents' advantage. Also you will have to go on the attack as there is no use playing long-drawn-out rallies; you will probably tire and make errors before the doubles pair. You need to try and outmanoeuvre the opposition by testing their team-work with accurate and, occasionally, surprising strokes.

This exercise is excellent for sharpening up your attacking strokes, your tactical ploys and your speed of movement. It certainly clears away any lethargy!

Doubles

Despite the fact that you have to consider the safety aspects of this game, it does give you the opportunity to broaden your tactical awareness. Since you now have four players on court the use of movement patterns has to be particularly sharp to keep you out of each other's way, and good ball control becomes even more important.

There are specifically designed enlarged courts for doubles play, but these are in such short supply that the majority of people use the conventional singles court. You can make the exercise safer by maintaining awareness of your opponents' positions at all times and, where necessary, by shortening your swing. The penalty point does not exist in doubles so if there is any doubt about player safety, stop the game immediately, and play a let.

43 Doubles is fun when not taken too seriously

44 Watching the ball is 'doubly' important where four people are playing in a confined space

This is intended to be a fun game rather than a seriously competitive one. The doubles teams must alternate strokes, thus giving them tactical options different to those of the singles game. Outmanoeuvring the opposing team is critical if there is to be some space into which a winner can be played. However, if the opponents play well as a team they will cover all areas of the court reasonably easily. Excellent ball control as well as accuracy and shrewdness of shot selection are essential for both sets of players.

TACTICS

Attacking play

Territorial advantage is particularly important in squash. You can gain the advantage over your opponent by taking up a position in the middle of the court and then selecting an appropriate shot to enable you to stay there. This means that your opponent will be forced to retrieve your accurate strokes from any of the four corners, making only the briefest of visits to the middle of the court. This is a very simplistic analysis of tactical play but it is a useful one to bear in mind.

The midcourt area is often referred to as the 'T' position due to the 'T' shape formed by the line markings on the floor. But do not be misled by this – your ideal position is approximately two feet deeper than the 'T' and closer to the back wall. The 'T' position takes you too far forward, requiring greater speed, reflexes and anticipation in the execution of the stroke. Failure to achieve this leaves you with

45   Phil Kenyon (England) takes up his position in the middle of the court and plays a good drive to the forehand to put Jahangir Khan (Pakistan) on the defensive

46 Del Harris (England) dives for the ball in his eagerness to overcome the challenge of Ashley Naylor (England)

poor-quality, loose strokes which give your opponent the advantage. Nothing is lost by adopting this alternative midcourt position, particularly if it enables you to make a better stroke and force a weak reply from your opponent. While it is always possible to move forward in order to attack, it is much more difficult to turn quickly and retreat to the back of the court in hasty defence.

The player dominating the middle of the court tends to hit the ball more accurately and does not tire as quickly as his opponent, who is forced to chase the ball from corner to corner. The player who spends the most time in the middle of the court usually ends up the winner; it is rare for the player doing all the running to win unless the match changes and he eventually gains the key position. Shot selection is crucial in determining who takes command of the middle of the court and the best shot is always the one that leaves the ball furthest away from where your opponent is standing.

The following is a tactical appraisal of some of the major strokes in squash which is designed to clarify the process of shot selection.

The back corner drive

This is usually referred to as a 'length', mainly because the ball is struck to the back corners so that it 'dies' on the second bounce at the back wall. To provide an effective counter to the drive the ball has to be cut off before it reaches its destination. This forms a great basis for the start of any rally. If in doubt, drive the ball straight down the wall to the corners. Try to hit straight drives rather than cross-court ones, because then your opponent will have to contend with the side wall in making his return and also he will probably have to cover a greater distance in order to retrieve.

The back corner drive nearly always puts great pressure on your opponent and hopefully will force him to play a defensive angle to the front court. Always be on the look-out for this, because then you may be able to play a winner and finish the rally victorious.

If the drive to one or other of the back corners does not have the effect of forcing the angle, at the very least it will remove your

opponent from the middle of court, allowing you to take up residence there. The ploy is also quite often the simplest way of putting together a very basic rally, and is used by many of the world's best players when they are seeking to play error-free squash while sparring for position.

It is tactically very shrewd to work a lob to

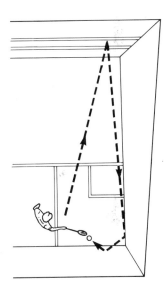

Fig 29   A length hit hard on the forehand up the side wall

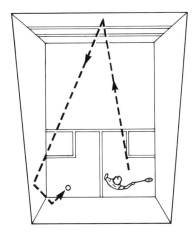

Fig 30   Back corner drive to gain position

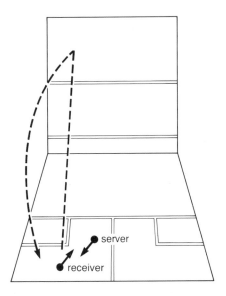

Fig 31   Lob to the back corners

the back corners into this framework in order to add variety and a change of pace to your basic game. The slower pace of the lob means that your opponent has less to hit at in the back corners, making the angle more difficult if not impossible and also giving you a base on which to build some attacking options. It is important to master this move before moving on to more ambitious tactics.

Front court play

The back corner drive should take your opponent out of the midcourt area into the back corner, so the next attack should be directed to the front of the court. This does assume that your opponent's returned stroke is less than perfect, allowing you to place the ball in the front court and so leave him stranded at the back. If this is not the case then continue to stroke the ball to the back corners and wait for the weak return. If you do receive the weak reply that you want, look to make your next stroke as low over the tin as possible and try to hit it towards the furthest front corner of the court. The following are three basic ways of finishing this rally.

1. *The kill* This hard hit stroke looks to all intents and purposes like a drive, so it has the

effect of making your opponent hesitate at the back of the court in case it comes straight back to him. It is too late for him to reach the shot by the time he realises that it has been struck much lower over the tin than he expected, and things are even worse for him if the ball finishes in the straight or cross-court nick. The risk of error is high, and so you will need to practise a great deal to build up confidence and to ensure the success of the stroke. Inaccuracy will result not only in your hitting the tin, but also, if you hit the ball too high, in a drive that will feed the ball straight back to your opponent – tactically not very desirable.

2. *The drop shot* The situation is the same as for the kill, but the ball has all the pace taken off it, keeping it short in the front court. Hopefully you will be able to play this touch shot with the same accuracy as the kill, that is hitting the ball as low over the tin as possible and aiming it at the nick either straight or cross-court. The drop shot, particularly the straight one, is the most lethal way of finishing the rally. It has been described as the most important stroke in squash.

3. *The angle* The situation is the same as for the previous two options; as before, keeping the ball low over the tin should make the shot effective. The one drawback with this stroke is that because it travels from the side wall to the front wall it takes longer to reach its destination, thus making it possible for your opponent to retrieve. However, since such a chase can be extremely tiring you could use this as a deliberate ploy to try and sap your opponent's physical strength. Also, since you can select either the normal angle or the reverse angle, the play may be used to keep your opponent guessing. It is probably better not to overplay this shot, but to use it sparingly when large distances of the court have to be covered by your opponent.

Volleying

So far you have used the back court drives to force the loose return for the front court winner. However, it may be that your opponent makes a good reply and strokes the ball down the wall or across the court. You must immediately assess whether the reply can be

47 Jansher Khan (Pakistan) improvises his footwork to manufacture a forehand drop shot

48 A moment's delay by Donna Vardy (England) allows Sarah Fitz-gerald (Australia) to disguise her shot

accurately vollied because of poor width or poor height. If you do decide to volley, then all the front court options listed before become available to you from your position in the middle of the court. Also, since the volley enables you to take the ball early in its flight, you will catch your opponent off-balance and still recovering from his previous stroke.

Many coaches exhort their player to 'take the ball early' as a means of increasing the pressure on the opponent. However, unless it is possible to play an accurate volley off a less than accurate stroke from behind, it is not a good idea to rush relentlessly around the court looking to volley everything; for one thing this is very tiring and you could run out of energy particularly quickly if you don't pace yourself.

The volley played at shoulder height is the best option for a winning stroke – anything higher or lower than that can be very difficult to control. Remember to practise all of these options until they become easier.

Deception

This is an advanced tactic which you will need to master as you reach a higher standard of play. So far all your strokes will probably be obvious to your opponent, both from the execution and from the pattern of your selection. This will allow your opponent to anticipate and read your game to such an extent that you will see him arrive at the next shot almost before you have hit the ball there!

It is important not to broadcast your intentions to an opponent, but to keep him guessing until the very last minute and then send him the wrong way by subtly changing the direction of your stroke. To do this you should take up a good position in the court, with your footwork and body position allowing you to select from the full range of strokes. Then you can make as if to hit one stroke and change it at the last minute. For example from the same position in the front court a straight drive to the back corner can be changed at the last moment to a short, sharp angle. If the opponent has just covered for the drive, he will have no chance of recovering and moving quickly forward to retrieve the stroke.

Another ploy you could use in the front court

is to show your opponent the straight drop, wait until you hear the footsteps committing him to retrieving it, and then at the last moment, turn the ball across the court. This is particularly embarrassing for your opponent, and if you can pull it off successfully it will have a marvellously unsettling effect on him, keeping him guessing and unsure as to what ploy is coming next. The element of surprise is always a good thing, and even if your opponent does manage to retrieve the ball, it is still very tiring to be wrong-footed in this way. Thus your opponent will be pressurised into making mistakes or at the very least prevented from reading your game and therefore mounting an attack on you.

49 Qamar Zaman (Pakistan), the master of disguise. Try guessing what he is doing here!

Attacking from the back court

So far the attacking moves have all come from the front court. This is because it is easier and safer to hit the ball low over the tin from the front court, and also because the attack is usually made in response to a poor reply from your opponent. But there is no doubt that if your confidence is high and your opponent has played an untidy ball into the back corners or the three-quarter court area, you should use your attacking range of strokes from these positions too in order to keep up the pressure. However, care and accuracy are vital in these areas, and if there is any uncertainty in your mind, concentrate on biding your time in the rally until you get a better opportunity.

You may have an opportunity to attack from the back court if there is a lively bounce or if an attempted drive to the back corners has poor width. The advantage of this ploy is that it will normally take your opponent by surprise, and he will realise that it is not enough simply to keep driving the ball deep into the back corners. This unsettling of your opponent can often signal the turning-point of a match one way or the other. However, you should avoid using this attacking ploy in desperation because it rarely works.

The counter-attack

In the rare event that a rally is not going all your way and you are having to defend, you should always be alert to the possibility of the counter-attack.

There is nothing more disconcerting than to be attacking your opponent only to find, when you play a less accurate stroke, that he seizes upon it immediately and hits a winner. This can easily happen if, for example, you have planned to finish the rally with a drop shot in the front court but your stroke ends up being too high and too loose. You could then be left stranded in the front of the court if your opponent rushes back and drives the ball fiercely to the back court. While this is an unpleasant experience when it happens to you, it is a marvellous counter-attacking weapon.

The 'counter' drop shot is another good ploy. Having played a drop shot to the front of the court your opponent will be so pleased with the

50 Sarah Fitz-gerald (Australia) playing a backhand out of the back corner

stroke that he will retreat to the midcourt area. Because you have anticipated the shot early and have moved quickly towards it you will be able to play a 'counter' drop shot to his stroke, thus causing him real problems when he tries to return to that part of the court.

You must learn to read rallies, to anticipate potentially weak strokes and to move in swiftly for the kill. Always be alert to the possibility of turning your defence into attack.

Defensive play

Defensive play is more difficult to allow for tactically, since it is a matter of survival. Having to retrieve puts enormous strain on your ball control and physical resources. More often than not you will not have much option as to which stroke to play, and it is more likely that you will strike the ball to the front wall any way you can. So long as the ball is still in play there is always a chance that your opponent may make a mistake.

The drive

There are certain strokes that are more difficult to attack than others. One of these is the drive hit deep to the back corners and close to the side walls. If you are not controlling the ball well this may cause you a problem, but if your side wall work is good you will be able to play your way back into a rally or even a match. A long rally containing twenty or more strokes to the back corner is the best way of stabilising your play and making it difficult for your opponent to sustain a 'purple patch' of winners.

51 Susan Devoy (New Zealand) forced to play defensively from the backhand back corner after a good stroke from Lucy Soutter (England)

The lob

The lob is another favoured method of resolute defence. The lack of pace combined with the great height of the stroke make it difficult to attack, and it slows down the whole pace of the rally. This allows the defending player to move to the middle of the court, forcing the attacker to make his reply from deep in the back corner. Even if he does manage to volley the lob, it is never easy to control the stroke accurately, and so the defending player may be let back into the rally. Also, it is very tiring for the opponent to be constantly stretching high to make the stroke.

Playing under pressure

In defence you are often required to play your stroke while at full stretch and off balance. Do not be overambitious; choose a stroke you know you can play without making an error. When under such pressure technique often collapses, resulting in your giving away easy points. However, as you reach higher standards of play your defensive skills will improve because you have to adjust to the elaborate attacking variations of more experienced opponents.

The first area to weaken under pressure is the cross-court shot, giving your opponent a great opportunity to volley a winner. Thus unless

52 Jansher Khan (Pakistan) shows exemplary footwork to play the lob off the backhand

53 Experienced England international Phil Kenyon is forced to improvise and play a shot behind his back in this match against his compatriot Brian Beeson

cross-court strokes are either very wide or very high they should not be hit at all, but should be replaced with a stroke hit straight down the wall to the back corner.

Finally, you should always chase your opponent's attacking strokes tigerishly and never give up the hope of retrieving them. Tactically speaking, one of the best ways to frustrate an opponent is to keep retrieving strokes that he believes are winners. He will invariably lapse into error if you keep harrying him.

Hand in/hand out

This refers specifically to the tactical implications of having the right to serve or not. With service you are able to score points, so it is right to adopt an attacking policy, because a winner will show tangible benefit to your score and an error will merely result in the loss of the right to serve.

When you are receiving service it is important not to become too safety-conscious, since if you play too negatively you will be easy prey for a more adventurous opponent. However, you should not be tempted to try an extravagant or risky winner either, as you will lose the point if it goes wrong. Play sensible squash when receiving service, do not give away easy points and be mindful of who is serving when you set out to choose the tactics for each rally.

Length of rally

If you have made your reputation as a fit, strong player who never tires and who rallies endlessly, play to your strengths – prolong the rally, retrieve everything and wait for your opponent to tire and make mistakes. You can achieve victory by exploiting your opponent's deficiencies and mistakes.

If, on the other hand, you have an array of accurate winners, use them to good effect; look for short rallies which you can finish with your winner and don't ever allow your opponent to control and draw out the rally.

To become a complete player you will have to be skilled in both these extremes and be able to dictate the precise length of a rally according to your tactical needs. Squash has been described as a sort of mobile chess, so you should keep varying your attacking and defensive moves, probing for a way through your opponent's resources. Remember to keep your mind open to ways of winning points at every stage of the game, make every stroke count and test your opponent to the full. Once you have mastered the fundamentals of stroke-making, getting to grips with the tactical side of the game is the real challenge of squash.

Mobility

Movement on the squash court is not natural but consists of a crab-like series of twists and turns. Ideally, you will be playing squash accurately enough in the tactical skirmish of a match not to have to stray too far from the middle of the court. In the event of your opponent being just as skilled and tactically adroit as you, then you will have to be prepared to run around the court retrieving his strokes.

Positioning

As we saw earlier, the ideal starting position for any movement is not the 'T', but a point approximately two feet further back in the court, closer to the back wall. All movement should start from here, since it is approximately central to all the corners of the court. Although it is slightly further towards the front corners of the court than the back, this is only due to the fact that it is easier to move forward to the front corners than it is to the back. Always try and return to the middle of the court except in the following circumstances.

(a) You may be under such pressure that you need to try and anticipate your opponent's next stroke, and so don't have enough time to return to the middle of the court (although you may pass through it at high speed).
(b) You are attacking your opponent and have played a good near-winning stroke. Your opponent then makes a loose return, and you go immediately to that part of the court to hit the winner. This is where returning to the middle of the court could waste vital moments, as your opponent is already out of position from his desperate defence.

A determination to stay in the middle of the court is vital if you are to win the match. Try and make the movement to the middle instinctive, so that you do not lose valuable time thinking about it.

Assuming that a movement from the middle of the court is required, there are certain key elements that you should take into account.

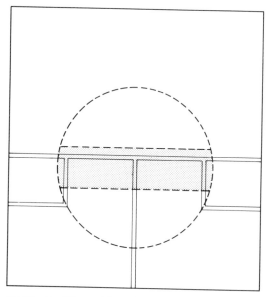

Fig 32   The 'T' area (shaded)

Watching the ball

By keeping your eye on the ball you can save yourself many unnecessary extra steps around the court to reach the point where you make

54 Jahangir Khan (Pakistan) shows perfect preparation for his angle from the back corner, while great rival Jansher Khan, also of Pakistan, waits in readiness in the middle of the court

your stroke. Do not make any premature movement until you have worked out where the next stroke is to be played. Running further than is necessary is both tiring and unintelligent. Learning to watch the ball allows you to be economical and more efficient in your movement towards the ball.

Footwork

Try and take short, economical strides and time them so that you arrive at the correct position for addressing the ball; overstriding will result in a loss of balance. Top-class players make footwork look easy, as though they have all the time in the world to reach even the most difficult of strokes. However, players of average standard are frequently condemned to overstriding due to the pressure applied by an opponent's good stroke play.

Balance

Assuming that all has gone smoothly in your movement towards addressing the ball, good balance should be easy to achieve, making the difference between a good stroke and a bad one. If you are off balance at the moment of striking the ball, you will find that you invariably make errors. Also, if you are less than controlled in your footwork, it will be difficult to keep your balance. This is precision work and only practice can make a natural instinct out of clumsiness. It is therefore useful to look back through all the skills practices concentrating this time on movement and balance.

Anticipation

It is not enough just to recover the ball and go back to the middle of the court. You must try to

55 Welshman Adrian Davies watches the ball intently in his encounter with England's Geoff Williams.

56 The author, although quite well balanced, has a troubled look in his eye

end each rally with a winning stroke, or at least remain in a state of readiness for the next play. Where possible, watch both the ball and your opponent closely and see if you can pick up any advance signs of where he is going to hit the ball. This is called reading the game and, when you become proficient at it, you will be able to steal valuable split seconds from your opponent by striking the ball earlier than he would want. Very often this ploy alone can win you the rally. However, do be careful because there is a thin dividing line between anticipating a play and just guessing, which can be disastrous. You will

find that your anticipation will improve with experience as you spend more and more hours on court.

It is worth noting that the better your anticipation becomes, the easier you will find it to maintain good footwork and balance. The essence of good movement around the court is to plot mentally the most direct route to the ball and the timing of your movement. Do not rush madly in the general direction of where you think the ball might land; be more specific and accurate in your movement.

57 Ross Norman (New Zealand) is on the move even before Jansher Khan (Pakistan) has hit the ball. If he has not anticipated correctly he will lose the point

58 Jansher Khan (Pakistan) lines up to play the forehand drop shot. His opponent Chris Dittmar (Australia) has already anticipated this move and is on his way to retrieve the ball

Pressure

You will be under a great deal of pressure if your opponent is spending more time in the middle of the court than you are. This could be potentially disastrous for you, and tactically the roles need to be reversed. It is important to stay calm and to try at all costs to avoid rushing in madly to retrieve the strokes. Of course this is easier said than done. You may possibly find, when faced with a desperate situation, that all the elements, perhaps fortuitously, come together to provide you with one chance to make an accurate or even winning stroke and so turn the tables on your opponent. However, if your footwork becomes erratic due to all the pressure, it is safe to assume that you will not be

able to do this without some amazing stroke of luck such as a mishit off the edge of the racket.

Do not allow your movement around the court to become ragged; if you do, your defeat will only be a question of time. The bottom line is that if you cannot regain access to the middle of the court, you will place extreme demands on your physical fitness and stamina because you will have to chase from corner to corner. There are two possible solutions to this problem. The first is to turn the tables tactically (which we dealt with elsewhere in the text), and the second is to follow physical conditioning programmes. The latter option will prepare you for a major feat of endurance, so that hopefully your opponent will grow tired of you scampering to get all his strokes back into play, and will ultimately make errors and lose.

FITNESS TRAINING

Getting the balance right

This aspect of squash tends to provoke much discussion and, in some, an obsessional attachment. There is no doubt that the world's top professionals will aim for the highest possible standards of fitness to gain the advantage over their opponents. At these standards of play, physical conditioning can make the difference between winning and losing, assuming that the players' skills are in equal proportion. However, it is no use being well-conditioned if, technically and tactically, you are not able to prolong the rally sufficiently to make the physical advantages pay dividends.

Therefore, long, stringent training sessions are not necessary until some degree of match-playing competence has been reached. Physical conditioning can only account for a small percentage of the improvements in your match play, whereas you can gain unlimited scope for improvement by concentrating on your racket skills and your tactical ploys.

Health considerations

If you are at all uncertain about your health, seek medical advice. Squash is a violent game which makes great demands on the human body. Being competitive will make you want to push yourself to the limits in pursuit of success in the sport, but this should never be at the expense of your health. Be sensible and enjoy the sport – don't try and be a hero because there will always be another day.

Of course, you do have to be fit enough to be able to get to the ball in order to hit it. If you are so overweight or unhealthy that this is not possible, then on medical grounds alone you should not be on the court. Before taking up squash you should make sure that you are sufficiently mobile to be able to master the basics of the sport. Then, by working systematically through the practice exercises and persevering with your match play, you should improve your mobility and fitness. Thus as your standard of play improves, so too does your level of fitness.

Tactical considerations

Some players base their whole tactical approach around their athleticism and fitness, so they have to train harder to compensate for their defensive attitude to the game. Tactically, such players are committed to chasing up their opponent's best strokes in an attempt to frustrate and force him into making an error. Many players who do not have the full range of strokes play this way, adding a great deal of interest to contests between skilful players and physical players since it is fascinating to see the stroke-maker try and win the match quickly in order to avoid losing a long attritional battle.

Fitness exercises

The following exercises constitute a training routine for those players who have the highest aspirations or who require an insight into what the best players do. A small section of this routine will suffice for those playing

59   **Zarak Jahan Khan (Pakistan) performs the splits, demonstrating his great athleticism**

recreationally, while if you are happy enough with your fitness and your game there may be no need to follow it at all.

Physical conditioning must concentrate on developing stamina, a good recovery rate, speed and agility. The model player must possess all of these elements, but by definition they do tend to pull in opposite directions. For example speed does not function easily with stamina, because one requires an explosive strength and the other a slower, enduring strength. Your objective should be to obtain a good balance and to adapt all of these ingredients to your style of play. Although more fun, you should not work exclusively on your strong points because it is your weaknesses that need the most attention.

Off-court forms of training

Distance running is the most basic way of developing increased stamina for squash. But it

should be noted that this form of training taken on its own will lead to 'heavy legs', and so should be confined largely to the off-season or to a sizeable break in your squash-playing programme. This is because while you may be able to last out in long matches, you may be too slow to keep up with the pace of the rallies. If you do use this type of training on its own, you will have to work hard to ensure that your speed is also being developed.

Build up a regular programme over one to three months, setting yourself a weekly target which should increase over the designated period from 15 miles (25 kilometres) per week to 25 miles (40 kilometres). Keep to a set number of miles each day, allowing yourself a couple of days off per week. Try to run on grass rather than hard surfaces, because with the slight give in the surface it is kinder to the body.

Other less bone-shaking means of achieving the same end include covering the equivalent distances by swimming or cycling, but the former may be ruled out because you cannot swim, and the latter may need longer distances to give you the equivalent work-out.

Skipping is normally considered the domain of the boxer, but it also has great value for squash players, not only to build stamina but to improve speed and co-ordination. If you do not co-ordinate your arms and legs properly, the exercise stops and you have to start again, ensuring good discipline. Aim to do 1,000 skips per day in 10 blocks of 100, but make sure you build up gradually to it. You can use this form of exercise in conjunction with your running, swimming or cycling, or use it as an alternative. A mixture of these four different aerobic exercises is the best since variety keeps boredom at bay. Training off the court is quite often not an attractive proposition to squash players, so try and keep it interesting. Always be constructively critical of your performances and don't cheat on yourself as there is only one loser.

Shuttle running

This is geared to improving your sprinting speed and recovery time. Mark out from your starting-line distances of 5, 10, 15, 20 and 25 yards (4.5, 9, 13.75, 18 and 23 metres). Next, sprint from the starting-line to the 5-yard mark and back again, then to the 10-yard line and so on until each distance is covered. On completing the 25-yard shuttle, take a rest of around two minutes at first, aiming to reduce this eventually to a minimum of 40 seconds. Try to do these exercises in groups of 10. If you want to do more groups, take a five-minute break between groups. The important points to remember are to give each run all you've got and also to turn as quickly and efficiently as you can. This agility will be a very useful asset when applied to movement around the squash court.

Sprint running

If you have access to a rugby field, this is a very useful area for practising sprint runs because the markings of the pitch are ideal. Start from one try-line and jog to the 22-metre line, then sprint from here past the half-way line on towards the 22-metre line in the other half of the field. Decelerate to a jog and finish at the try-line at the opposite end of the field. Walk back to the 22-metre line, jog to the half-way line and then complete the distance by sprinting from the half-way line to the try-line from which you started originally.

The emphasis is once again on giving your all for the sake of speed, using the jogging and the walking as a means of recovery. The sprint, the jog and the walk form one unit, and you should try to build up to blocks of ten or fifteen repetitions. Concentrate on quality not quantity speed so that you can take a breather between each sprint as and when it is needed.

You can develop this exercise most effectively by climbing a short hill at a sprint. Approximately the same distance should be covered and once again you should aim for maximum speed as you go to sprint. The incline makes you drive harder for speed, while sprinting the section downhill calls for balance and control.

All the exercises so far have been off-court for the simple reason that court time is valuable, and if you are paying for it you should always maximise the opportunity to improve racket skills. However, there are some players who like to do their physical work on the court.

Court training or ghosting

This exercise simulates movement on the squash court, making use of the racket but not the ball. Start from the 'T' position and then move towards each of the four corners of the court in turn, always returning to the 'T' after visiting each corner. Next, move towards the service-box side wall immediately to the right of the 'T' and then to the left. Thus the exercise consists of six different moves and each time you arrive at one of the destinations, you make as if to play the stroke that would be required in that situation – hence the term 'ghosting'.

However, some would say that this is not a good practice as far as movement around the squash court is concerned. Unless the ball is present it seems too easy to cheat (although this may not be intentional). The imaginary stroke-making is of no real use other than as a part of the overall work-load. Nevertheless, there is great value to be gained from this exercise, particularly if you have nowhere else to go for your training.

There are two different uses of the ghosting technique. The first is as a stamina and recovery-rate exercise. For this you run to each of the six points on the court outlined earlier for a period of forty seconds before going back to the 'T' and then resting for another forty seconds. You may find in the early stages that you need a longer rest, but aim to match the work time to the resting time. Forty seconds should be enough to enable you to make about twelve visits to different corners, but ultimately you should aim to improve this number. Repeat the whole exercise in batches of ten. This should simulate the effects of a hard rally so the more you can improve your resting or recovery rate, the more effectively you will be able to continue playing coherent squash undiminished by the effects of fatigue.

The second use of the ghosting technique is to produce speed. Plot a course so that you visit all of the six corners and go back to the 'T' between each run, but do the course only once at top speed. Then immediately take a rest, allowing yourself sufficient time to recover so that you are fresh and raring to go each time. If the course takes fifteen seconds to complete, you should take sixty seconds to rest. This can be done in groups of twenty. The emphasis here is on speed and agility, and quality of performance is preferred to quantity.

It is very useful to work on the speed, stamina and recovery-rate elements which we have covered here in combination with the practices for racket and ball outlined earlier. Remember, however, that you will have to have a good degree of proficiency in racket and ball skills to achieve a high enough work-rate to tax yourself physically.

The warm-up

The human body is very similar to a car in some respects since you cannot expect it to perform efficiently at top speed from the very first moment. Most of the world's top sporting performers go through all kinds of stretching and light jogging exercises in order to warm up prior to launching themselves at their maximum capacity. They also perform a similar routine at the end of their match, and this is called warming down. Both warming up and warming down are extremely important if you are to avoid injuries and stiffness in the muscles, but also if you want to do your very best. There are many types of exercise which may be used and you must select a short programme that is suitable for *your* needs.

The following are two particular exercises for the lower back region – that part of the body which takes most of the strain during a squash match or practice session.

Sit-ups

You will probably be familiar with this exercise. Perform it lying on your back with your knees raised, your feet on the floor, and your arms behind your head. Pull yourself up to the correct position with your head forward. There is no real need to hurry this exercise; try to feel the stretching effect on the back and to make the most of it. Perform the exercise in groups of twenty continuous sit-ups.

Back stretches

This time lie flat on your stomach with your arms behind your head. Raise your head and feet just a few inches off the ground. Once again feel the stretching in the lower back and don't rush. This exercise should be done in groups of five.

These two exercises in conjunction with your other exercises should leave you well prepared to go and do battle on court. After the match don't forget the warming-down process, since this helps to prevent stiffness and soreness overnight. This is particularly important if you have to play again the next day, which is why it is rarely forgotten by the professionals.

Training for squash is never an easy thing to structure around your fixture list, but it is prudent to do most of the heavy stamina and recovery-rate work during the off-season. While working on speed and agility is reasonably compatible with your match play, remember that rest is just as important if you are to be sufficiently fresh to reap a rich reward for your hard work. If you are overworked and under-rested you will not be hungry and fresh for the contest.

MATCH PREPARATION

We must look now at the preparations that need to be made on the final countdown to your big match. All the hard work in practice and in training will have been done, and this will be the last phase in ensuring that all of your stringent efforts reap a rich reward and produce the winning formula. Pre-match nerves will play a part, and there is a great deal that can go wrong during the crucial period between the end of practice and training but before the appointed time for your match.

Tapering

As in most sports where strenuous physical effort is needed to provide the basis for a good performance, it is necessary to apply what is sometimes called the tapering effect. This simply means taking a rest and freshening up your appetite for the competition to come so that even when you have trained hard and are suffering from fatigue, you will be hungry for the fray. That hunger alone can win you points, because it gives you the advantage in terms of speed, mental alertness and a positive attitude towards playing your best squash. You don't necessarily have to stop going on court to practise, but you do have to avoid heavy physical work, placing the emphasis instead on racket skills and ball control with only light physical involvement.

One school of thought maintains that tapering should mean a complete break from your squash work, but this may upset your routine and can only work if you have a steely confidence that you can play your best squash

after the break. Hence most people will prefer to scale down the sessions so that the routine is maintained. A few days' break should be quite sufficient as too long a break may allow your nerves to jangle and you will have fewer doubts if you keep yourself occupied.

Diet

During tapering you pay particular attention to your physical condition and it becomes increasingly important to eat well. A balanced diet with regular meals is normally sufficient, but if you want more specific advice for your own requirements, then consult a dietician or your general practitioner. Looking after your body's nutritional needs is vital if you are to achieve your best physically and also if you are to have the confidence to play well. A junk food diet would give you no such confidence, although it is all too easy to become sucked into eating such food during a tournament because meals of good nutritional value are not always provided. You should therefore try to make your own arrangements for meals, helping you to gain a useful psychological advantage over your opponent.

The timing of your meals is also of vital importance. You should never attempt to play on a full stomach; either allow yourself plenty of time to digest your food or eat only light meals until after you have played. Re-scheduling matches can play havoc with any carefully planned routine and tournament organisers often get into trouble with players for disrupting their set eating times.

Sleep

Sleeping habits are also important. The key is to stick to a routine, keep regular hours and avoid late nights. However, there are no hard and fast rules because if you are feeling nervous before a match you may well find yourself lying awake, playing and replaying the match over and over again in your mind. You should sleep soundly whenever you can in order to build up a routine that you can follow in such situations.

It is hard to argue against partying and late nights given that some great sportspeople have put in their most remarkable performances after a night of indulgence. Some would claim that enjoying yourself in such a manner helps to keep your mind occupied and relaxed, leaving you better prepared to commit yourself totally to your match the next day.

This aspect of preparation is a personal thing which you should work out for yourself. Generally, however, the more routine approach is overall the most advantageous. You could spend the night before the match enjoying a good meal in the early evening (so that it can be fully digested), and then visiting the cinema or hiring a video, before going to bed at the usual time. You should then get a good night's sleep and wake up fully prepared for your big day.

Match-day preparation

On the day of the match there are two key things you can do. The first is to go to the court where you will be playing your match and practise there for between twenty minutes and half an hour. The object of this is that you become familiar with the court and how it plays for pace, providing you with the basic confidence to stay calm during the hours before your match, and allowing you to work through your strokes and perfect your timing. Also, it gives you the opportunity to warm up in preparation for later on in the day.

The second thing to do is to check that your travel arrangements bring you to the club in plenty of time for your match. All your meticulous preparations will be worthless if, when you arrive, you are forced to change

quickly and rush on to the court. If you are late you will tend to lose your composure, and because you will not have had time to warm up correctly you will make a sluggish start to your match. This often results in your opponent taking the first game off you, something that you really don't want to happen. If you work out your travel arrangements properly, you should be within striking distance of the venue the night before, particularly if it is a long distance away. Therefore, taking into account the local conditions and your route, you should set off early enough so that if there is a traffic problem you will still arrive on time. Remember that players are often scratched from major events because they turn up late.

Assessing your opponent's abilities

The first real chance you will have to assess your opponent is in the course of the knock-up. This is the prelude to the match and lasts five minutes. Normally you will hit forehands for half of that time and backhands for the rest.

You should concentrate on three main objectives. Firstly, aim to slot straight into your groove, concentrating on accuracy, timing and control. Secondly, make sure that you are moving smoothly and efficiently towards the ball, thus preparing yourself for the harder work to come during the match. Finally, test out your range of strokes in order to gain some clues from your opponent as to how he will respond to them. Of course this will not give you a very accurate guide; although your opponent may sometimes play a particular stroke badly during the knock-up because he is concentrating on his timing, once the match begins his play may improve dramatically.

However, if you lob the ball to your opponent and he volleys it on the forehand for a dead nick, you can be sure that he is strong in this area. On the other hand, if you hit the lob to the backhand side, resulting in a tin, then you may assume that this is a weak area of your opponent's game. Look for these clues throughout the knock-up and, most importantly, during the match itself.

Dealing with an opponent's strengths

If you do find a particular strength in your opponent's game, then obviously you should try and avoid feeding it. However, while it is often easy to identify an opponent's favourite and most successful shot, it is less easy to play away from that part of the court where it is usually hit because your opponent will probably create the opening for himself. Do avoid feeding the strong shot at all costs, or at least try supplying the stroke with more or less pace than your opponent would really want. This is often sufficient to make the opportunity less straightforward, and at best may turn the favourite shot from a lethal weapon into a source of weakness and error.

Exploiting weaknesses

When you have identified a weak area of your opponent's game, look to exploit it. However, beware that in seizing upon this weakness you do not end up attacking that area relentlessly, because ultimately it will cease being a weakness. Your opponent will have come under such pressure in the supposed weak area that eventually he will have the chance to correct and perfect it to such an extent that it may well become a strength.

What you should do, therefore, is to play your normal game and try to pick on the weakness when your opponent is most vulnerable. For example a lob may exploit a vulnerable backhand volley, catching the opponent out of position or off balance, and making the stroke even more difficult for him. Also, since some players are weak at the front corners on the drop shot, you should try encouraging them to play this stroke when they are not fully in position by seeming to hang back in the court. If this is an uncertain stroke in their repertoire they are likely to accept the challenge and take the risk, usually leading to an error. Keep your mind alert to such possibilities and always look to exploit any openings that occur with a view to gaining tactical superiority in the rally.

Assessing your own abilities

The tables can easily be turned in this situation as no self-respecting opponent is going to allow you to attack his weaknesses and play away from his strengths without doing the same to you. Therefore, you must begin to recognise for yourself the weak areas in your game, both so that you can work hard on them in practice, but also so that you can play away from them in a match. Do not be anxious to prove your versatility in your weak areas; just play steady and sensible strokes to defend them. If in doubt, a good drive down either side wall will certainly be the best option, and you should also look for the opportunity to play one of your killing strokes. This should come naturally, but if you become too ambitious or careless do not be afraid to play more steadily; the simplest and easiest strokes are always the most effective.

Once you have established a winning formula by playing to your own strengths and to your oponent's weaknesses, do not change it but keep on milking your winning strokes for all they are worth.

Loss of form

Every player experiences a loss of form some time in their career, and yet often no one can explain why. This loss of form can last for a few points, a few games, a few matches or even a few weeks or months. It happens to many sportspeople, but the important thing to remember is not to panic, which would only aggravate the situation. Of course this is easier said than done, but one thing you can do is to focus on the basics of the game, particularly if this loss of form happens at the start of your match.

Batsmen in cricket are often instructed to play themselves in before they try to hit the ball out of the ground. Similarly, in squash you should play yourself in gradually before attempting to win rallies with your most extravagant and skilful strokes. You can do this by hitting the ball to the back corners down each wing of the court, providing you with the rhythm and the confidence to try more difficult strokes.

This certainly ensures that you don't give away too many points by playing your full range of strokes before you are hitting the ball cleanly.

You must not be disheartened if things begin to go astray in the middle of a match. There is no player around that can play to his best all the time. You must ride out the bad patches by moderating your tactical ploys and stroke selection as there is usually scope to come through a bad patch in a match and end with the right result if you stay calm. If the reason you are not winning matches is inconsistency, then this is a more difficult matter because you will have lost confidence, making the prospect of your regaining your winning form unlikely.

In order to overcome this difficulty you must go back to the fundamentals, work hard to correct your mistakes and also consult your coach. To re-establish a winning formula, select opponents of a lower standard so that you regain your form before going back to face your normal level of opposition. Loss of form can occur for many reasons but most often because of pressures outside the court, such as problems in your domestic life, your work life and even in your social life, as well as the obvious problems of injury. These problems are never very easy to solve, and they can have a dramatic effect on your squash.

A good way of trying to maintain consistency in your game is to carefully plot your season around well-conceived aims and objectives. If you work on the premise that you won't play at your peak in every match in every event, then it is important to select certain key events in the year for which you aim to be at your very best. You should set yourself a target whether this is promotion in the club league, or a county, national or world ranking. It is important to work hard to achieve these fixed goals, and to measure your improvement against them. Most players will aim for an improved ranking by gearing their play to a specific event. Even if your main aim is to beat your neighbour before the end of the season, that may be sufficient stimulus to bring the best out of you. You will find that this targeting enables you to focus and progress steadily towards your goal, making the ups and downs seem less critical than if you were playing aimlessly.

In the same way that you must create objectives for yourself, it is a good idea to keep a 'little black book' with a note of all matches, scores and results. Also, if it is at all possible, keep notes on your opponents' strengths and weaknesses; the observations you make will always come in useful if you have to play that opponent again, and it means that you will not be blindly taking on a new opponent each time. Although it is true that your opponent may well have improved since you made your notes, nevertheless it does give you an interesting base from which to start the match.

Mental preparation

You will probably have gathered by now that all the regular practice routines, the training and the meticulous preparatory work is geared towards one thing – to allow you to give of your best in a match situation. Nobody likes to lose their matches and if you have prepared well physically you should have the confidence to walk on court with a positive mental attitude. Matches are won and lost on mental attitudes alone, thus being in the correct frame of mind is vital.

You will find it a pleasure to play on those days when your confidence is high and all your strokes fall into place to provide you with sufficient winners to carry the day. However, there will be days when you have to be determined that you can still win the match even though you may have started badly because of your own mistakes or because your opponent is on top of his game. You must maintain a positive attitude in the belief that if you persevere and try to play your normal game, you will still have the ability to win at the death. It is easy to become dispirited and lose your way, but the end result is that your basic game becomes littered with mistakes and you give the match away to your opponent. You must at least make things difficult for your opponent, forcing him to earn every point. If you are able to prolong the rallies and the match lasts quite a long time, even though you may start badly there is always time for you to recover your best form and turn the tables on your opponent.

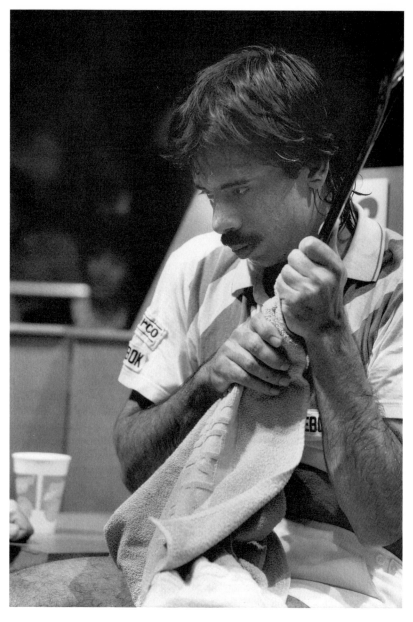

60 A quiet moment during a match is a rare thing. Jahangir Khan (Pakistan) uses his time between games to good effect, gathering himself mentally and steeling himself to win the match

Squash may be described as a battle of wills and considerable strength of mind is required at the highest levels. The saying 'there is no gain without pain', seems to sum up the sort of mental attitude necessary to the game especially when you are confronted by an opponent of some repute. It is vital that you play each match against your opponent and not against what may be a considerable reputation. You will have to believe in your own capabilities if you are to have any chance of success. Don't allow yourself to become overawed by your opponent's game or concede mentally by playing at less than your very best. The bottom line is that if you make your opponent earn his victory then you will at least have gained a valuable lesson from experiencing the differences between his standard of play and yours.

61 Zarak Jahan Khan (Pakistan) enjoys good natured banter with the referee during his match

Accepting the referee's decisions

The referee is always likely to find it difficult to make good decisions, particularly ones that suit both players all of the time. However, you must try to accept these decisions, not only when they are in your favour, but also when they are not. If you do not adopt such an attitude, it can seriously affect your concentration and therefore your performance in the rallies that follow. There is certainly no point in allowing one bad decision to adversely affect your chances for the next few rallies. Some people claim that over a period of time the decisions will average out until the good ones equal the bad. You need to be able to display great self-restraint and discipline, so that you are at an advantage when your opponent sees you coping calmly with the effects of bad refereeing decisions. Often matches can be won or lost depending on the way in which you or your opponent handle the decisions given.

Perseverance

In the final analysis you must always adhere to the philosophy that a match is never won until the final point has been claimed. There are many tales of everything going wrong for the player who is first to reach match point, so you must maintain a positive attitude and see the match through to its end. If you are ahead, do not stop concentrating until a win has been called by the marker and the referee. On the other hand, if you are losing do not despair or concede the game even at match point down – many a match has been won at this stage. You should dig deep for greater reserves of determination in order to turn what appears to be abject failure into a startling success.

RULES AND SAFETY

Up to now I have concentrated on factors which will make it possible for you to improve your game. However, it is also necessary to have a good working knowledge of the rules and etiquette of the sport. I do not propose to deal with the rules of the sport specifically (these are to be found in the Squash Rackets Association's rules booklet) but to dwell on certain aspects of the rules that may need interpretation.

The basic rules of the sport are not difficult and are obvious even to beginners. The difficulty arises concerning the ability of a player to be able to move around the court and strike the ball with minimal physical interference from his opponent. Such traffic problems can be exacerbated by a player who is able to manipulate the situation so that he blocks the most direct route to the ball or subtly crowds the swing, thus causing his opponent to make errors. This professionalism is not easy to detect but it can have a dramatic effect on the outcome of the game.

It is no wonder therefore that officials have a difficult task unravelling the mysterious advantages to be gained by clever use of the traffic flow during the rally. The close proximity of the two contestants on court can make the game scrappy and untidy since sometimes the players seem more concerned with achieving a form of physical superiority rather than trying to outplay each other using racket skills and good tactics.

62 In this situation the referee would allow a let to avoid any traffic problems

The officials

The two officials in charge of the match have quite different responsibilities.

The marker

As the name implies, this involves keeping the score and announcing the beginning of the match. The marker controls the overall flow of the game, calling faults and checking that all the basic rules of the game are enforced. He makes no decisions on lets, penalty points or contentious situations. He merely announces the decisions that are made and ensures that the game continues according to the rules and the interpretations of them that are made. The role is relatively straightforward but by no means easy.

The referee

This is the most difficult of jobs. The task here is to ensure that there is always a correct and fair outcome both to the individual rallies and to the end result. If the players do not agree a call of fault from the marker, they have final right of appeal to the referee. His assessment has three possible outcomes – it can be positive, negative or, if he is unsure or unsighted, a let.

The referee has control of the timekeeping of the games and the knock-up and, most importantly, ensures that play is continuous. He is in the hot seat for the course of the match and is in the direct line of fire of the players. The referee can make one of three decisions which will keep the game flowing.

1. *No let* This is when the referee considers that there is no good reason for replaying the rally since there was no physical interference. Thus it is obviously possible to continue playing the rally unless, of course, a winner has been played. Each player is obliged to make every effort to play the ball at all times.
2. *The let* This is the call that allows the rally to be replayed. The referee decides that there has been an accidental collision of players, the one player attempting to get out of the way to allow his opponent to move to the ball and make his stroke. Usually the ball will have been played accurately and the players will have become unintentionally entangled. The rule allows both players access to the ball in turn, giving them a fair chance to stroke the ball.
3. *The penalty point* This is a more complex situation. The referee has to decide whether there has been deliberate interference or, alternatively, whether such a bad stroke has been played that the player is unable to move out of the way of a possible winner. The decision seems straightforward at face value, but it is extremely vulnerable to subjective interpretation, particularly among the three interested parties. The referee's ability to make the right decision will soon be assessed by the two players, and there will be every opportunity to exploit the situation if one or other of the players feels he can do so to his advantage. However, if the players are playing the game in the right spirit it is the continuity of the game which will be the important thing.

Since the sport of squash is becoming increasingly competitive it is important that the referee is able to read the tactical intentions of the two players. If he cannot do so then he will probably not be able to ensure fair play because he will unwittingly be giving the advantage to one of the two players. It has to be remembered, however, that there are players who do not move fluently around the squash court, and that allowances have to be made for this failing. But at the same time there is a thin dividing line between what is permissible and what is clearly a tactical ploy used to gain the upper hand.

There will inevitably be some players who use this subtle 'blocking' tactic as a means of compensating for their own inability to make winning strokes. Instead of winning rallies cleanly, this type of player will try to force errors from you by making it difficult for you to get to the ball and make your stroke. Thankfully, as standards of racket skills in the game improve, the dependence on these physical tactics seems to be decreasing. Nevertheless, such tactics seem to be inherent to the game, particularly at critical points in a match, because it is almost as if the two players are on the same side of the tennis net competing against each other. There is nothing more untidy to watch than a squash

63 **Having played a backhand drop shot Jahangir Khan (Pakistan) makes little effort to allow Rodney Martin of Australia to retrieve the ball**

match full of penalty points and lets, and both players should, in the interests of the game, try to keep the rallies flowing so that the more aesthetically pleasing aspects of the game such as racket skills and tactics can come to the fore.

Improving standards

With standards of play in the game constantly improving, it is important that refereeing standards are also raised. It is a useful exercise to try and do your fair share of marking and refereeing, as spending some time in the hot seat will teach you how difficult the task is. It also helps you to gain a better understanding of how the game appears from the referee's seat, and is useful to the game in the long term, since players should take responsibility for controlling matches. Squash is a player's game and the players know best how they want the rules interpreted. Never be afraid to officiate – it is good for you and it is good for the game.

If refereeing standards in the game are low at the moment, then the main reason for this is the lack of agreement between referee and players as to how the rules should be interpreted. Very few ex-players become officials, and thus the views of players and officials tend to diverge.

Code of conduct

The referee's decisions have been given additional strength by the recently implemented code of conduct for the sport. It is necessary to implement this where the two parties involved do not agree, and it is mainly intended to ensure the smooth running of the professional game and its tournaments. However, there is evidence that county leagues have begun to enforce penalty points for behavioural problems as well. It is clear that more work needs to be done to make certain that the rules of the game are interpreted soundly and thus that a fair result is the norm.

Safety aspects

There are certain risks attached to playing squash, but the dangers can be reduced by observing a certain combination of etiquette and common sense. Certainly both the racket and the ball can be lethal weapons simply by virtue of the fact that the players are frequently very close to each other when they play the ball.

The ball

The most serious risk of injury is to the eye. The ball can penetrate the eye socket and so potentially cause untold damage. However, by taking some simple safeguards it is possible to avoid playing yourself into such a dangerous situation. The first thing to remember is to watch the ball at all times. More often than not it is when you are looking round to see where the ball is that you leave yourself open to a blow in the face. If you keep your eye on the ball you should be able to tell when your opponent is going to hit the ball in your direction, thus enabling you to take the correct evasive action instinctively.

One particularly dangerous situation occurs when you have positioned yourself in the middle of the court and the ball is inaccurately struck into the back corner. The tendency here is to watch the front wall, but this does not allow you to anticipate the next move and when you feel that your opponent's stroke is slow in coming you will probably turn around to see what has happened – usually precisely at the moment when the ball is struck. Watching the ball is a vital ingredient in your overall concentration and is absolutely necessary if you are to anticipate your opponent's next stroke.

You should do everything possible to avoid hitting your opponent with the ball as it leaves a very painful mark. When this happens accidentally it is excusable with an apology, but where there is deliberate intent to harm the opponent a match can deteriorate into a nasty physical confrontation. If you get a reputation for foul play it is likely that you will find that few opponents volunteer to play against you. It should not be necessary to hit your opponent and it certainly does nothing to improve the spirit of the game.

If you do hit your opponent then, assuming that the ball was on its way to the front wall, it is your point. However, if you repeat the exercise then you may suffer a warning for dangerous play, and also incur the wrath of your opponent. Where the ball was travelling to the side wall, as in the case of the reverse angle, then a let is the result. It may be that your opponent is hogging the middle of the court after playing a poor shot to the back corner. Rather than stroking the ball at your opponent, it is good etiquette here to show the stroke that you want to play and stop to ask for a let on the grounds that the direction in which you wanted to hit the ball was blocked by your opponent. The referee will then inform your opponent that he is crowding and ask for the rally to be replayed as a let. This leaves all the parties involved unscathed and also avoids any unpleasant or intimidating play.

The racket

Graphite composite rackets are very strong and nearly unbreakable, so if you are hit by one it will definitely do you some damage. As before, it is not wise to swing the racket excessively, particularly when your opponent is close at hand. However, it is possible to achieve a territorial advantage by taking a full swing, especially if your opponent has played a weak stroke which lands in the centre of the court. It is necessary to distinguish between taking an excessive swing in order to force your opponent out of position and taking a reasonable swing even when crowded. The important thing is that in both cases the opponent should not be hit by the racket. Again, you must remember that,

64 Jahangir Khan (Pakistan) sees the wisdom of backing off just sufficiently to let Ross Norman (New Zealand) play his stroke

while accidents do happen, hitting your opponent should never become a tactical ploy. If there is any doubt about the safety of a stroke, then you should always ask the referee for a let. The referee can penalise an excessive swing or crowding with a penalty stroke if he believes that the situation warrants it.

Aggression

There is no reason why you should not play with aggression and enthusiasm, but this should always be within the bounds of the rules and also in line with the spirit of the game.

Turning

Another situation that can cause concern is that of turning. This is mainly a problem in the back corners, more often than not on the return of service. The most common instance occurs when the ball is served to the backhand corner. The ball hits the side wall and falls on to the back wall, catching the player receiving service out of position with the bounce. The opponent is unable to step backwards and play the backhand return because the ball has gone past too quickly, so he has to spin round rapidly and collect the ball with the forehand from a

65 Martine Le Moignan (England) displays the kind of aggression that won her the world title

position in the middle of the court near the back wall. Thus because the server is forced to stay in the service box for fear of being hit by the ball, this leaves the rest of the court open for his opponent to drive the ball away for a winner. However, if, as you should do, you have moved to the middle of the court after the service, you will either have to stand and take the punishment or hope your opponent is courteous enough to seek the let.

The technique for the return of service should rarely necessitate turning and there should be no need to hide from playing the backhand unless you are a beginner. If you find that you are employing the turning technique a great deal, then it would be most useful to get a coach to teach you how to avoid it. Turning is not a very popular ploy and if you use it too often you may find that you are running short of opponents very quickly or that your matches become very intimidatory and hostile.

Some new rules

There is an evolutionary process taking place in squash rules which is largely motivated by the desire to make the sport appealing to a wider audience, particularly through the medium of television. These changes are designed to make the game more entertaining for the arm-chair audience.

Scoring

The most obvious change that has been tried is the new scoring system. According to the old system you can only score a point when you are serving or are 'hand in' and in order to serve you have to win a rally 'hand out'. Thus you have to win two rallies to score your first point. A criticism of this scoring system is that it is not easy to follow or understand. International squash tournaments have, for the most part, changed to the American scoring system. In this system points are scored by the winner at the end of each rally, and the total number of points required to win a game is fifteen and not nine. This makes the contest clearer to the spectator, but whether it changes the tactical

mechanics of a squash match for better or worse is yet to be decided.

The tin

Critics of the game argue that rallies are long and boring because the ball is constantly being driven to the back corners from a safe height on the front wall. Players retort that if they risk attacking strokes which are low over the tin, their opponents are so finely tuned physically that they can reach the ball often with apparent ease. The International Squash Players' Association have therefore opted in selected tournaments to experiment with a tin that is lower than normal – 17in (43cm) from ground level to the top instead of 19in (48cm). The traditionalists don't like it and the visionaries have not yet proved the success of the experiment, but it has certainly provided the squash world with some interesting food for thought.

Time-periods in matches

Another recent development in the rules states that the knock-up at the start of each match should be shared and no player should be allowed to knock-up on his own. Also, the time-period for rest between games has been tentatively increased.

The service

The service has been made slightly more difficult in that now players have only one service chance – any fault results in the loss of the rally. This change is designed to ensure that players pay more attention to the service because hitherto it had been treated with contempt as merely an easy way of putting the ball into play at the start of the rally. The change will not have a dramatic effect on the game, but it will make players take greater care.

These newer additions to the rules may not be with us for long, but they are helping in the development of the game. It is encouraging to see some of the great minds in the sport looking for improvements and developments.

CONCLUSION

In the same way that, at the end of a game of squash, conclusions must be drawn if you are to advance and improve, so we must now attempt constructive analysis of what has gone before.

The elements of the game

We have seen how the game of squash is a combination of separate elements; strokes, tactics, positive mental attitudes and good physical attributes. If you can blend all of these elements together, you will be well on the way to playing high-calibre squash. I have deliberately listed the qualities in order of importance, although it is not easy to rigidly distinguish between them. Certainly, the primary requirement is to have the necessary ability to execute the strokes and to use them in an ordered fashion which gives you a sound strategical approach. If you then marry these two elements to a positive mental approach, you have the game's challenges at your disposal. There is no limit to how much you can improve if you focus on these areas, but squash should also be a great source of fun and a pleasurable social activity for those whose aspirations are not geared to the very highest levels. Physical fitness is always very important, but should not be overemphasised. As was stated earlier, while it does help to be in good physical shape, this should not be the only requirement for successful squash.

Previously, it was the physical and persevering players who were able to gain the upper hand against the amateurish skills of the more stylish players, but in the modern game most matches are decided more on racket skills and determination. This has been an evolutionary process and has caused much relief among the students of the game because, during the period of the game when the physical aspects were dominant, it did make for a rather long and attritional style of play that was tedious in the extreme for the unfortunate spectator. The modern player is having to search for more skilful ways of winning rallies, and this has had the effect of making the game more entertaining for the spectator. Whichever style of play you favour you must not become completely dependent on one element of the game alone. The better you become in all of these areas, then the more dramatic will be your overall improvement.

Older squash players

No matter what your age, it is always possible to play better squash, particularly if you master the tactical art of stroke-making which will enable you to avoid much of the physical strain of chasing around the court. When they first arrive on the scene, many players chase the ball without too much thought, but as they mature they try to make sure that their opponent does the running by judiciously placing their strokes.

Thus it is possible to play the game to a ripe old age, as witnessed by Hashim Khan who was competing around the world with great success in the over-55 category when he was well into his 60s. Other well-known players, such as former world champion Geoff Hunt, who is in his forties, are capable of giving away vital years to their opponents and still be skilful enough to contest matches with a reasonable chance

66 Hiddy Jahan (England) looks on in amazement as his opponent, Abbas Kaoud (Egypt) becomes airborne. These two seasoned campaigners still manage to keep their audience entertained

of success. The vital requirement when you get older is that you should continue to appreciate the fun of the game as well as the need to go on learning and meeting the challenge of squash.

The future

Squash is played around the world by an ever-expanding number of people. It is by degrees becoming a more desirable spectator sport as facilities improve and there is more coverage of squash on the television. The increased involvement of commercial companies in sponsoring events is a welcome investment in the game's future, particularly as regards the professional tournaments, and the best players in world squash are now attaining the same high profile as other sportspeople do in their respective fields.

The court

The court is the most obvious area of technical development. Some twenty years ago it was considered revolutionary to replace the back wall of the court with a specially toughened glass wall. This considerably increased the number of spectators and also made it possible to introduce seating where previously there was standing room only.

The court has now become almost like a goldfish bowl, and is made of glass, perspex or plastic. To prevent the players becoming distracted, high-density lighting has been introduced inside the court while the auditorium is kept in darkness. In addition, some of the walls of these courts are treated to give added visibility to the players. Thus the court creates quite a spectacle, described by one eminent journalist as an extraterrestrial cube of light. This type of court can be moved around, which means that it can be installed in some of the great sporting venues such as the Wembley Conference Centre or the Royal Albert Hall. These transparent courts do not have quite the same playing characteristics as the traditional plaster-wall courts, but the modern player enjoys having a platform on which to demonstrate his skills.

Television

Television has not been slow to recognise such technological advances as the transparent court, but changes have had to be made to the ball because previously it was barely visible on the television screen. Thus we now have what is known as the 'teleball' which has the ability to light up on the screen. This is a ball constructed in a similar way to a golf ball, with reflective material inserted in the dimples of the ball's surface. To create the necessary brightness on screen, a light is placed on top of the camera lens to help trace the path of the ball both for the benefit of the camera and, ultimately, the viewer.

67 The 'teleball' is made like a golf ball but it has dimples which are illuminated when light hits their reflective surface

Television has also had an impact on the colours traditionally associated with the sport; clothing now often incorporates pastel shades and cosmetic changes have been made to the court, including colouring the floor dark blue or green and making the lines yellow.

However, despite the efforts made to attract them, television companies are still not entirely convinced that squash makes good viewing, nor have they yet mastered the art of presenting an interesting programme of recorded highlights.

The claim is that the best players make the game look infinitely more easy than it actually is, while greater drama is necessary to cater for the needs of the television viewer. The rules have been tinkered with in an attempt to increase the drama of the game, but there is a danger that the events that are specifically tailored for the timing constraints of television either lack the excitement of the traditional game or are so confined as to make the game unrecognisable because players are no longer able to perform to their expected standards. It is also said that squash is still a minority sport, which all goes to explain why there are so few matches shown on television for the enthusiasts. The advent of cable and satellite television stations may help to improve the situation, but the sport must also learn to package itself better and provide more events which will be of interest to the viewer.

The concept of squash as a spectator sport for television is a relatively new one, and given time there is no doubt that the game will be able to attract mainstream interest. Innovators in the sport will clearly not rest until such a breakthrough has been made.

INDEX